Company's Coming®

VEGETABLES

by
Jean Paré

Cover Photo

1. Layered Vegetable Loaf page 116.
2. Cream Sauce page 86.

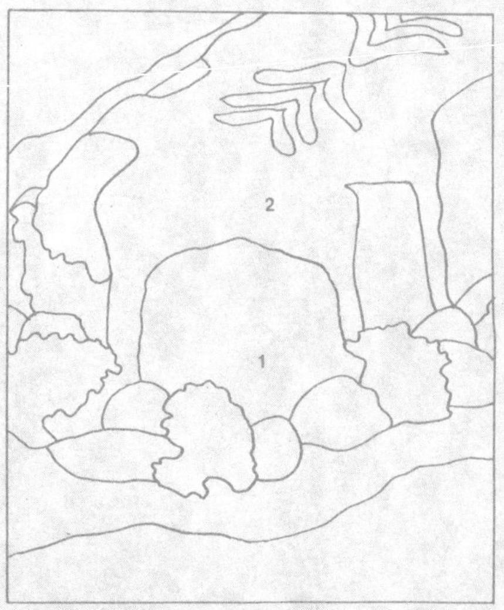

VEGETABLES

First Edition April 1989

I.S.B.N. 0–9693322–0–3

Published and Distributed by
Company's Coming Publishing Limited
Box 8037, Station "F"
Edmonton, Alberta, Canada
T6H 4N9

Printed in Canada

Cookbooks in the Company's Coming series by Jean Paré:

150 DELICIOUS SQUARES

CASSEROLES

MUFFINS & MORE

SALADS

APPETIZERS

DESSERTS

SOUPS & SANDWICHES

HOLIDAY ENTERTAINING

COOKIES

JEAN PARÉ'S FAVORITES
VOLUME ONE

VEGETABLES

MAIN COURSES (SEPT. 1989)

table of Contents

the Jean Paré story

Jean Paré was born and raised during the Great Depression in Irma, a small farm town in eastern Alberta. Jean grew up understanding that the combination of family, friends and home cooking is the essence of a good life. Jean learned from her mother, Ruby Elford, to appreciate good cooking and was encouraged by her father, Edward Elford, who praised even her earliest attempts. When she left home she took with her many acquired family recipes, her love of cooking and her intriguing desire to read recipe books like novels!

While raising a family of four, Jean was always busy in her kitchen preparing delicious, tasty and savory meals for family and friends of all ages. Her reputation flourished as the mom who would happily feed the neighborhood.

In 1963, when her children had all reached school age, Jean volunteered to cater to the 50th anniversary of the Vermilion School of Agriculture, now Lakeland College. Working out of her home, Jean prepared a dinner for over 1000 people which launched a flourishing catering operation that continued for over eighteen years. During that time she was provided with countless opportunities to test new ideas with immediate feedback – resulting in empty plates and contented customers! Whether preparing cocktail sandwiches for a house party or serving a hot meal for 1500 people, Jean Paré earned a reputation for good food, courteous service and reasonable prices.

"Why don't you write a cookbook?" Time and again Jean was asked that question as requests for her recipes mounted. Jean's response was to team up with her son Grant Lovig in the fall of 1980 to form Company's Coming Publishing Limited. April 14, 1981 marked the debut of "150 DELICIOUS SQUARES", the first Company's Coming cookbook in what soon would become Canada's most popular cookbook series. Jean released a new title each year for the first six years. The pace quickened and by 1987 the company had begun publishing two titles each year.

Jean Paré's operation has grown from the early days of working out of a spare bedroom in her home to operating a large and fully equipped test kitchen in Vermilion, near the home she and her husband Larry built. Full time staff has grown steadily to include marketing personnel located in major cities across Canada and the United States. Home Office is located in Edmonton, Alberta where distribution, accounting and administration functions are headquartered.

Jean Paré's approach to cooking has always called for easy-to-follow recipes using mostly common, affordable ingredients. Her wonderful collection of time-honored recipes, many of which are family heirlooms, are a welcome addition to any kitchen. That's why we say: taste the tradition.

Color your meals with vegetables.

foreword

Vegetables are often given too little thought when planning a meal. It may be that cooks are somewhat at a loss when attempting to think of more creative ways to serve vegetables. Help is at hand!

Vegetables are best served freshly cooked. Most cooked vegetables do not freeze well due to loss of texture. To avoid overcooking test by poking with the tip of a sharp paring knife rather than a fork. A fork will tend to break vegetables apart at a point when they are already overdone.

To retain vitamins, cook vegetables in a small amount of water. Bring to a boil, covered. Lower heat and simmer slowly until tender. A bit more water may need to be added to prevent burning. It is ideal to have very little water left to drain. The French method of cooking green vegetables keeps the color bright. They are boiled, covered with water, in an open saucepan. When tender crisp they are drained and cooled under cold running water. They are kept chilled and sautéed as needed.

A small amount of granulated sugar, as little as ½ tsp. (2 mL), does wonders for all vegetables when added to the cooking water, especially those that have not been freshly harvested.

In this book you will find the most common to the not-so-familiar vegetables with a host of different ways for preparing and serving. A few of the recipes call for meat, but they are adaptable as vegetarian dishes should you choose. Try Special Baked Potatoes, Baked Mushrooms and Classic Carrot Ring, to name a few favorites.

Servings given are approximate. So much depends upon the size and the number of vegetable varieties being served with the meal.

Let vegetables make the difference with your next meal - company's coming!

Jean Paré

SPINACH STUFFED TOMATOES

Colorful and good. Use tiny tomatoes for an appetizer.

Tomatoes	**8**	**8**
Salt, sprinkle		
Frozen chopped spinach	**2 × 10 oz.**	**2 × 284 g**
Butter or margarine, softened	**¼ cup**	**50 mL**
Chopped onion	**1 cup**	**250 mL**
Grated carrot	**½ cup**	**125 mL**
Chopped celery	**½ cup**	**125 mL**
Chopped green pepper	**½ cup**	**125 mL**
Eggs	**2**	**2**
Milk	**½ cup**	**125 mL**
Seasoned dry bread crumbs	**1 cup**	**250 mL**
Salt	**1 tsp.**	**5 mL**
Pepper	**¼ tsp.**	**1 mL**
Parsley flakes	**1 tsp.**	**5 mL**
Grated Parmesan cheese (or use Cheddar)		

Cut off tops from tomatoes. Scoop out pulp. Sprinkle tomato cups with salt. Turn upside down to drain.

Cook spinach according to package directions. Drain well.

Put butter, onion, carrot, celery and green pepper into frying pan. Sauté until onion is soft and clear. Add spinach and remove from heat.

Beat eggs until frothy. Add milk, bread crumbs, salt, pepper and parsley. Mix with spinach mixture. Stuff tomatoes.

Sprinkle with cheese. Arrange in greased baking pan. Bake uncovered in 350°F (180°C) oven for 20 to 25 minutes. Serves 8.

Pictured on page 17.

No matter what they say, lightning never strikes the same place twice. After one strike the same place isn't there anymore.

ARTICHOKE PIE

Good flavored pie. Just right for a luncheon.

Pie crust pastry, your own or a mix, see page 113.		
Butter or margarine	**2 tbsp.**	**30 mL**
Chopped green onions	**¼ cup**	**50 mL**
Canned artichoke hearts, drained and quartered	**14 oz.**	**398 mL**
Sliced mushrooms, drained	**10 oz.**	**284 mL**
Eggs	**4**	**4**
Cream or milk	**1½ cups**	**350 mL**
Salt	**½ tsp.**	**2 mL**
Pepper	**⅛ tsp.**	**0.5 mL**
Garlic powder	**¼ tsp.**	**1 mL**
Grated mozzarella cheese	**½ cup**	**125 mL**
Grated Swiss or Cheddar cheese	**½ cup**	**125 mL**
Hot pepper sauce	**⅛ tsp.**	**0.5 mL**

Line 9 inch (22 cm) pie pan with pastry.

Melt butter in frying pan. Add onion. Sauté until soft. Remove from heat.

Add artichoke hearts and mushrooms. Put into pie shell.

Beat eggs in bowl until frothy. Mix in remaining ingredients. Pour into pie shell. Roll out pastry for top. Moisten edge. Cover with pastry. Press to seal. Trim. Cut several slits in top. Bake in 350°F (180°C) oven for 40 to 50 minutes until browned. Cuts into 6 pieces for a meal or into 12 pieces for appetizers.

VEGETABLE STUFFED MUSHROOMS

It's amazing how tasty vegetables can be in a stuffing.

Medium mushrooms	**12**	**12**
Butter or margarine	**¼ cup**	**50 mL**
Mushroom stems, chopped		
Finely chopped onion	**¾ cup**	**175 mL**
Finely grated carrot	**¾ cup**	**175 mL**
Finely chopped celery	**2 tbsp.**	**30 mL**
Seasoned salt	**¼ tsp.**	**1 mL**

(continued on next page)

Gently twist stems out of mushroom caps.

Melt butter in frying pan. Add remaining ingredients. Sauté until vegetables are softened. Remove from heat. Stuff mushroom caps. Arrange on broiling pan. Broil until sizzling hot. Makes 12.

Pictured on page 17.

POTATO SKINS

Great as a snack or an appetizer.

Small potatoes, baked	**6**	**6**
Medium Cheddar cheese strips, cut smaller than potato skin	**12**	**12**
Grated Parmesan cheese, good sprinkle		
Chopped chives, good sprinkle		
Grated mozzarella cheese, thick layer		
Paprika		

Cut potatoes in half lengthwise. Scoop out pulp leaving shell ¼ inch (6 mm) thick.

Lay cheese strip on each skin. Sprinkle with Parmesan cheese. Sprinkle with chives. Top with mozzarella cheese. Sprinkle with paprika. Arrange on baking sheet. Bake in 350°F (180°C) oven for 10 to 12 minutes. Makes 12 skins. To make smaller skins for finger food cut each half into 4. Makes 48 pieces.

Pictured on page 17.

SOUR CREAM DIP

Sour cream	**1 cup**	**250 mL**
Cream cheese, softened	**4 oz.**	**125 g**
Bacon bits	**2 tsp.**	**10 mL**
Onion flakes, crushed, or chives	**1 tsp.**	**5 mL**

Mix all ingredients together. Serve with Potato Skins. Makes 1½ cups (375 mL).

Pictured on page 17.

SPINACH TARTS

Serve hot as an appetizer or snack. A sure hit.

PASTRY		
Butter or margarine, softened	**½ cup**	**125 mL**
Cream cheese, softened	**4 oz.**	**125 g**
All-purpose flour	**1 cup**	**250 mL**

Beat butter and cream cheese together until smooth. Work in flour. Shape into long roll. Mark off, then cut into 24 pieces. Press into small tart tins to form shells.

FILLING		
Egg	**1**	**1**
Grated Cheddar cheese	**½ cup**	**125 mL**
Cooked chopped spinach, well drained	**½ cup**	**125 mL**
Sour cream	**¼ cup**	**60 mL**
Milk	**¼ cup**	**60 mL**
Salt	**¼ tsp.**	**1 mL**
Onion salt	**¼ tsp.**	**1 mL**

Beat egg until frothy. Stir in remaining ingredients. Spoon into shells. Bake in 350°F (180°C) oven for about 20 to 25 minutes until set. Makes 24.

Pictured on page 17.

SAUERKRAUT SNACK

Serve on toast for a snack or on crackers or melba toast for an appetizer. Unusual and good.

Cream cheese, softened	**4 oz.**	**125 g**
Grated Cheddar cheese	**½ cup**	**125 mL**
Onion powder	**¼ tsp.**	**1 mL**
Caraway seeds	**¼ tsp.**	**1 mL**
Granulated sugar	**1 tbsp.**	**15 mL**
Sauerkraut, drained	**14 oz.**	**398 mL**
Buttered toast or crackers		

(continued on next page)

Mix first 5 ingredients together well.

Add sauerkraut. Stir. Spoon on top of toast. May also be served in a small bowl to be spooned onto crackers. Makes about 2 cups (450 mL).

Note: Rinse and drain sauerkraut for a milder flavor.

Pictured on page 17.

ARTICHOKES

An uppity relative of the common thistle, choose heads with tightly clinging leaves. Stem should be firm. It should seem heavy for its size. Allow one medium artichoke per person. A fun vegetable which is really not as difficult to prepare as you may think.

Globe artichokes	**6**	**6**
Water		
Lemon juice	**2 tbsp.**	**30 mL**

To cook, cut off stem. Break off small leaves at the bottom. Slice ¾ inch (2 cm) from top. With scissors, trim tips from leaves. Gently spread leaves open. Remove silky fuzzy pulp (the choke) with tip of spoon and discard. Wash under cold running water. Place in single layer, each resting on its base, in enamel pan such as a small roaster. Do not use aluminum as it will cause them to darken. Pour water into pan about 3 inches (7.5 cm) deep. Add lemon juice. Cover. Boil for 30 to 40 minutes until tender when pierced with tip of paring knife.

Serve with Lemon Butter. To eat, remove outer leaf with fingers. Dip bottom of leaf into Lemon Butter, and pull through your teeth to scrape off soft pulp. Eat leaves in this manner. When you reach the heart (bottom), use knife and fork to finish. The heart is the best part.

LEMON BUTTER

Butter or margarine	**½ cup**	**125 mL**
Lemon juice	**2 tbsp.**	**30 mL**
Worcestershire sauce	**½ tsp.**	**2 mL**

Melt together. Ready for dipping.

Note: Alternate dips are garlic butter, herb butter, Hollandaise Sauce (page 84), mayonnaise or any other dip you feel like trying.

TOMATO FANS

A quick and easy last minute addition to any menu. A dieter's delight.

Firm ripe tomatoes	**4**	**4**
Cottage cheese	**1 cup**	**225 mL**
Chives	**1 tbsp.**	**15 mL**
Salt, sprinkle		
Pepper, sprinkle		
Lettuce leaves	**4**	**4**

Cut out stem ends of tomatoes. Turn upside down. Cut tomato into ½ inch (1.25 cm) slices downward being careful not to cut all the way through.

Mix cottage cheese, chives, salt and pepper together. Spread tomato apart. Stuff with cheese.

Serve on lettuce leaves. Serves 4.

Variation: Make 2 slits in cherry tomatoes. Insert cheese circles or smaller amounts of above cottage cheese mixture.

Pictured on page 17.

RICE STUFFED TOMATOES

Looks good and tastes good. Cheese adds much to the flavor. Makes good finger food when using small tomatoes.

Firm ripe tomatoes	**6**	**6**
Tomato pulp		
Cooked rice	**2 cups**	**450 mL**
Granulated sugar	**½ tsp.**	**2 mL**
Salt	**¾ tsp.**	**4 mL**
Pepper	**⅛ tsp.**	**0.5 mL**
Basil	**¼ tsp.**	**1 mL**
Oregano	**⅛ tsp.**	**0.5 mL**
Garlic powder	**⅛ tsp.**	**0.5 mL**
Parsley flakes	**½ tsp.**	**2 mL**
Grated Cheddar cheese	**½ cup**	**125 mL**

(continued on next page)

Cut off tops from tomatoes. Scoop out pulp and reserve.

Mash reserved tomato pulp. Add remaining ingredients. Mix together. Stuff tomatoes. Arrange in greased baking pan. Bake uncovered in 350°F (180°C) oven for about 20 to 25 minutes. Serves 6.

Pictured on page 17.

CHILIES RELLENOS CASSEROLE

Never was a Chilies ree-AY-nohs casserole so easy. Cheddar cheese rather than the usual Monteray Jack gives a superb flavor.

Canned chopped green chilies	**4 oz.**	**114 g**
Medium Cheddar cheese	**½ lb.**	**225 g**
Eggs	**2**	**2**
Milk	**2 cups**	**450 mL**
All-purpose flour	**½ cup**	**125 mL**
Salt	**1 tsp.**	**5 mL**
Pepper	**⅛ tsp.**	**0.5 mL**

Spread chopped chilies with juice in 8 × 8 inch (20 × 20 cm) casserole or pan. Slice cheese and layer over top.

Combine remaining ingredients in blender. Blend smooth. Pour over casserole. Bake uncovered in 350°F (180°C) oven for about 45 to 50 minutes until set. Casserole will test done if you insert a knife and it comes out clean. Serve hot as a side dish or cold as an appetizer. Serves 6 to 8 regular servings or cuts into 25 squares for appetizers.

Many horror stories are bought by bald men hoping for a hair raising tale.

VEGETABLE PIZZA

Make this as cheesy as you like as well as adding more or less of your favorite things.

Tea biscuit mix	**1⅛ cups**	**275 mL**
Milk	**¼ cup**	**50 mL**
Spaghetti sauce	**¼ cup**	**50 mL**
Grated mozzarella cheese	**1 cup**	**250 mL**
Chopped green pepper	**2 tbsp.**	**30 mL**
Sliced mushrooms	**¼ cup**	**50 mL**
Finely chopped onion	**2 tbsp.**	**30 mL**
Pitted black olives, sliced	**5 - 6**	**5 - 6**

Mix tea biscuit mix and milk together to make a soft dough. Pat onto greased 9 inch (22 cm) pan. Bake in 375°F (190°C) oven for 15 minutes to partially cook.

Spread spaghetti sauce over crust.

Sprinkle cheese over top. Sprinkle with green pepper, mushrooms, onion and sliced olives. Bake in 375°F (190°C) oven for about 15 minutes until hot and cheese has bubbled up through toppings. Cuts into 6 medium size wedges.

Pictured on page 71.

1. Parsnip Cakes page 74
2. Rice Stuffed Tomatoes page 14
3. Phyllo Triangles page 109
4. Spinach Stuffed Tomatoes page 9
5. Vegetable Stuffed Mushrooms page 10
6. Tomato Fans page 14
7. Sour Cream Dip page 11
8. Vegetable Kabobs page 19
9. Spinach Tarts page 12
10. Sauerkraut Snack page 12
11. Roasted Carrots page 23
12. Potato Skins page 11

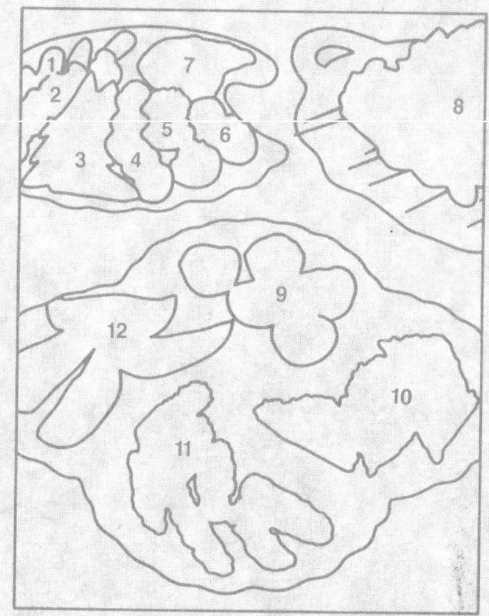

VEGETABLE KABOBS

Such a showy display. A knockout!

Carrot slices, ½ inch (1.25 cm) thick	**8**	**8**
Small onions, peeled	**8**	**8**
Salted water		
Cauliflower flowerettes	**8**	**8**
Zucchini slices, unpeeled, 1 inch (2.5 cm) thick	**8**	**8**
Whole mushrooms	**8**	**8**
Green pepper pieces, 1½ inch (4 cm) square	**8**	**8**
Red pepper pieces, 1½ inch (4 cm) square	**8**	**8**

SAUCE

Spaghetti sauce	**1½ cups**	**375 mL**
Vinegar	**¼ cup**	**50 mL**
Cooking oil	**2 tbsp.**	**30 mL**

Simmer carrot and onions in salted water for about 5 minutes.

Add cauliflower. Simmer 5 minutes more. Drain. Cool.

Arrange vegetables on 4 skewers on broiling pan. Brush with sauce. Broil 4 inches (10 cm) from heat for about 7 minutes. Brush with sauce and turn often. Makes 8.

SAUCE: Mix all together in bowl.

Variation: Sauce may be omitted. Brush vegetables with butter before, during and after broiling. Sprinkle with salt and pepper before serving.

Note: Cherry tomatoes make a good addition. The length of skewers will determine the number of vegetables which may be added. Large onions can be cut into squares to replace small onions.

Pictured on page 17.

The best way to look young is to stay around really old people.

SOUR CREAM BROILED TOMATOES

White topped tomatoes make a splashy entrance. Tasty as well.

Large, firm, ripe tomatoes	**4**	**4**
Sour cream	**½ cup**	**125 mL**
Mayonnaise	**½ cup**	**125 mL**
Salt	**½ tsp.**	**2 mL**
Pepper	**⅛ tsp.**	**0.5 mL**
Parsley flakes	**1 tsp.**	**5 mL**
Basil	**½ tsp.**	**2 mL**
All-purpose flour	**2 tsp.**	**10 mL**
Granulated sugar	**1 tsp.**	**5 mL**

Cut tomatoes in half crosswise. Squeeze gently to remove juice and seeds. Broil 6 inches (15 cm) from heat for 5 minutes.

Mix remaining ingredients together. Spread over tomatoes. Broil about 2 minutes more until tinged a golden color. Serves 8.

Pictured on page 89.

SESAME BROILED TOMATOES

Make ordinary tomatoes extraordinary. Delicious nutty flavor.

Large, firm, ripe tomatoes	**4**	**4**
Grated Cheddar cheese	**½ cup**	**125 mL**
Dry bread crumbs	**½ cup**	**125 mL**
Water	**3 tbsp.**	**50 mL**
Sesame seeds	**1½ tbsp.**	**25 mL**
Salt	**½ tsp.**	**2 mL**
Pepper, sprinkle		
Granulated sugar	**1 tsp.**	**5 mL**

Cut tomatoes in half crosswise. Gently squeeze to remove seeds and juice. Broil 6 inches (15 cm) from heat for 5 minutes.

Mix remaining ingredients together. Sprinkle over tomatoes. Broil 2 minutes more. Serves 8.

Pictured on page 89.

CRUMB BAKED TOMATOES

Dress up tomatoes ahead and pop into the oven when ready.

Large, firm, ripe tomatoes	**4**	**4**
Butter or margarine	**3 tbsp.**	**50 mL**
Dry bread crumbs	**½ cup**	**125 mL**
Parsley flakes	**½ tsp.**	**2 mL**
Salt	**½ tsp.**	**2 mL**
Pepper, sprinkle		
Granulated sugar	**1 tsp.**	**5 mL**

Cut tomatoes in half crosswise. Gently squeeze out seeds and juice.

Melt butter in small saucepan. Add remaining ingredients. Mix well. Divide among tomato tops. Arrange in greased baking pan. Bake uncovered in 350°F (180°C) oven for 25 to 30 minutes. Serves 8.

STUFFED TOMATOES

Bread crumbs are mixed with cheese, spices and tomato pulp to make this stuffing. Moist.

Large, firm, ripe tomatoes	**4**	**4**
Salt, sprinkle		
Pepper, sprinkle		
Dry bread crumbs	**1 cup**	**250 mL**
Grated Parmesan cheese	**¼ cup**	**60 mL**
Parsley flakes	**1 tsp.**	**5 mL**
Basil	**½ tsp.**	**2 mL**
Oregano	**¼ tsp.**	**1 mL**
Tomato pulp		
Butter or margarine, melted	**¼ cup**	**60 mL**

Cut tomatoes in half crosswise. Scoop out and reserve pulp. Sprinkle tomato halves with salt and pepper.

In small bowl mix bread crumbs, cheese, parsley, basil and oregano with reserved pulp.

Add melted butter to crumb mixture. Stir to mix. Spoon into tomato halves. Arrange on greased baking sheets. Bake in 350°F (180°C) oven for about 20 minutes. Serves 8.

MUSHROOM STUFFED TOMATOES

This is first choice for stuffed tomatoes. The choice of two spices poses a slight problem as both are splendid additions.

Medium tomatoes, red and firm	**8**	**8**
Salt, sprinkle		
Butter or margarine	**¼ cup**	**60 mL**
Chopped mushrooms	**6 cups**	**1.35 L**
Chopped onion	**½ cup**	**125 mL**
All-purpose flour	**1 tbsp.**	**15 mL**
Sour cream	**1 cup**	**225 mL**
Dry bread crumbs	**¼ cup**	**50 mL**
Parsley flakes	**1 tsp.**	**5 mL**
Salt	**1 tsp.**	**5 mL**
Pepper	**⅛ tsp.**	**0.5 mL**
Granulated sugar	**½ tsp.**	**2 mL**
Thyme (or use twice as much basil)	**⅛ tsp.**	**0.5 mL**
Dry bread crumbs	**¼ cup**	**50 mL**
Butter or margarine	**1 tbsp.**	**15 mL**

Cut off tops from tomatoes. Scoop out pulp. Sprinkle inside tomato cups with salt. Turn tomatoes upside down to drain.

Melt butter in frying pan. Add mushrooms and onion. Sauté until onion is clear. You may have to do this in 2 batches.

Mix in flour. Stir in sour cream then next 6 ingredients. Stuff tomatoes.

Mix crumbs with butter in saucepan over medium heat. Sprinkle over top. Arrange in greased baking pan. Bake in 350°F (180°C) oven for about 20 to 30 minutes. Serves 8.

Pictured on page 89.

Never be kind to a termite. They will eat you out of house and home.

ROASTED CARROTS

A bit fiddly but once prepared they can rest in the refrigerator for hours. For a crispy mottled appearance use crushed cornflakes. For a smoother look use fine cornflake crumbs.

Small whole carrots or larger ones, cut up	**1 lb.**	**500 g**
Water	**2 cups**	**500 mL**
Granulated sugar	**1 tsp.**	**5 mL**
Salt	**½ tsp.**	**2 mL**
Melted butter	**¼ cup**	**60 mL**
Crushed cornflakes	**½ cup**	**125 mL**

Cook carrots, water, sugar and salt together until tender. Drain. Cool.

Dip carrots into butter then into crumbs. Place on greased baking tray. Bake in 350°F (180°C) oven for about 10 to 12 minutes. Serves 3 to 4.

Pictured on page 17.

CHUNKY OVEN FRIES

A nice rich brown color, these have a minimum of fat. Rather than chunks, potatoes can also be cut into typical shape of fries.

Baking potatoes, peeled or unpeeled	**6**	**6**
Cold water to cover		
Cooking oil	**¼ cup**	**50 mL**
Paprika, sprinkle		
Salt, sprinkle		

Cut potatoes in half lengthwise. Cut each half into 4 pieces. Soak in cold water for 30 minutes, to remove starch and avoid clumping. This step may be omitted if desired. Drain. Blot dry.

Put cooking oil into bowl. Add potato pieces. Stir well to coat all pieces. Arrange on baking tray in single layer.

Sprinkle with paprika. Bake in 475°F (250°C) oven for about 20 minutes. Turn after 12 minutes to brown other side.

Sprinkle with salt and serve. Makes 6 servings.

VEGETABLE STUFFED PEPPERS

Corn, tomatoes, celery and onion fill these pepper cups. Make ahead and bake when needed.

Green peppers, medium	**3**	**3**
Boiling salted water	**4 cups**	**900 mL**
Bacon slices, cooked and crumbled	**4**	**4**
Niblet corn, fresh or frozen	**2 cups**	**450 mL**
Canned tomatoes	**14 oz.**	**398 mL**
Chopped celery	**¼ cup**	**50 mL**
Chopped onion	**¼ cup**	**50 mL**
Salt	**½ tsp.**	**2 mL**
Pepper	**⅛ tsp.**	**0.5 mL**
Grated cheese, tomato slice and grated cheese, buttered crumbs, bacon (half cooked) or tomato slice with buttered crumbs in center for topping		

Cut peppers in half crosswise. Remove seeds. Boil covered in salted water for 5 minutes. Drain.

Put next 7 ingredients into saucepan. Simmer slowly uncovered until celery and onion are tender, about 10 minutes. If mixture is too runny, add a little minute rice. Remove from heat. Cover and let stand 10 minutes. Stuff peppers. Arrange in casserole or small roaster.

Top with your choice of toppings. Cover. Bake in 350°F (180°C) oven for about 15 minutes. Remove cover. Bake 5 minutes longer. Serves 6.

BAKED POTATO TOPPING

A yummy topping, cheesy and flavorful.

Medium potatoes, baked	**6**	**6**
Butter or margarine, softened	**¼ cup**	**50 mL**
Grated Cheddar cheese, medium or sharp	**1 cup**	**250 mL**
Chopped green onion or chives	**2 tbsp.**	**30 mL**
Sour cream	**⅔ cup**	**150 mL**
Salt	**¼ tsp.**	**1 mL**
Pepper, light sprinkle		

(continued on next page)

Gently roll baked potatoes. Potholders will be needed. Cut cross in top. Press ends upward. Center of potato should push up.

Mix butter and cheese together. Add onion, sour cream, salt and pepper. Stir. Taste for salt and pepper. Scrape into small bowl. Pass with potatoes. Makes a scant 2 cups (450 mL) topping for about 6 potatoes.

BROCCOLI TOPPED POTATOES: Cook frozen chopped broccoli. Drain well. Spread on top of potato, lay part or whole cheese slice over top. Reheat in oven to melt cheese.

BAKED POTATOES: Mature potatoes should be used. Prick skins to allow steam to escape. For softer skins, rub with fat. Wrapping with foil produces a wetter potato. Place on oven rack. Bake in 400°F (200°C) oven for 45 to 60 minutes depending on size. Test with tip of sharp knife. Cooking longer at a lower temperature gives a thinner, softer skin. Cooking less time at a higher temperature gives a thicker, crisper skin. Roll gently before serving to produce a mealier product.

SPECIAL BAKED POTATOES

The prettiest stuffed potato going. Looks so rich and appetizing.

Baking potatoes	6	6
Potato pulp		
Butter or margarine, softened	**½ cup**	**125 mL**
Grated cheese	**1 cup**	**250 mL**
Light cream or milk, hot	**1 cup**	**225 mL**
Onion salt	**½ tsp.**	**2 mL**
Garlic salt	**¼ tsp.**	**1 mL**
Salt	**½ tsp.**	**2 mL**
Chopped green onion	**¼ cup**	**50 mL**

For crunchy skins bake potatoes as is. Wrap in foil or rub with fat for soft skins. Bake in 400°F (200°C) oven for 45 to 60 minutes until tender when poked with a sharp paring knife. Cut in half lengthwise.

Scoop out pulp into bowl being careful not to break skins. Add next 6 ingredients. Mash together.

Stir in green onion. Stuff shells. Arrange on baking sheet. Bake in 350°F (180°C) oven until hot. Serves 10 to 12.

ROAST POTATOES

Get a roast potato flavor with or without a roast of meat.

Potatoes, medium size, peeled	6	6
Water		
Butter or margarine	1 tbsp.	15 mL
Cooking oil	1 tbsp.	15 mL
Salt, sprinkle		
Pepper, sprinkle		
Paprika, sprinkle		

Boil potatoes in water for 10 minutes. Drain.

Heat butter and cooking oil in casserole or small roaster, large enough to hold potatoes in single layer.

Place potatoes in pan, turning once to coat with butter mixture. Sprinkle with salt, pepper and paprika. Cover. Bake in 375°F (190°C) oven for about 45 minutes until tender. Serves 6.

ROAST POTATOES WITH MEAT: Parboil potatoes for 10 minutes. Drain. After draining potatoes, place them around roasting meat about 45 minutes before meat is cooked. Sprinkle with salt, pepper and paprika. If you don't use a cover, you will need to baste potatoes when you baste the meat. Potatoes may be added without parboiling in which case you will need to allow at least 1 hour for cooking.

CHEESE STUFFED ZUCCHINI

This resembles a quiche filling in a zucchini base.

Zucchini, 6 to 7 inches (16 to 18 cm) long	6	6
Salted water		
Eggs	2	2
Grated medium Cheddar cheese	1¼ cups	300 mL
Cottage cheese	½ cup	125 mL
Dry onion flakes	2 tsp.	10 mL
Parsley flakes	2 tsp.	10 mL
Salt	½ tsp.	2 mL
Pepper	⅛ tsp.	0.5 mL

(continued on next page)

Cut ends off zucchini and cook whole in boiling salted water for 10 to 12 minutes. Should be firm but tender. Remove from water. Cut in half lengthwise. Scoop out pulp leaving some next to skin. Put pulp into bowl. Invert zucchini to drain on paper towels.

Add eggs to pulp. Beat well with spoon. Add Cheddar cheese, cottage cheese, onion, parsley, salt and pepper. Mix together. Fill each shell. Arrange in greased baking dish. Bake uncovered in 350°F (180°C) oven until browned, about 15 to 20 minutes. Serves 6 to 8.

SIMPLE STUFFED POTATOES

Simply mashed potato with cheese topping. Easy and delicious.

Medium potatoes, baked	**8**	**8**
Potato pulp		
Butter or margarine, softened	**¼ cup**	**60 mL**
Rich milk, hot	**1 cup**	**225 mL**
Salt	**1 tsp.**	**5 mL**
Pepper	**⅛ tsp.**	**0.5 mL**
Grated medium Cheddar cheese or cheese slices		

Cut ¼ inch (6 mm) slice lengthwise from potatoes.

Scoop out pulp into bowl. Add butter, milk, salt and pepper. Mash together. Spoon into potato shells. To make shells fuller, bake 1 or 2 extra potatoes to add to stuffing.

Sprinkle with grated cheese or cut slices into 4 triangles. Overlap 4 on top of each potato. Place on baking sheet. Bake in 400°F (200°C) oven for about 15 minutes until hot. Serves 8.

There is only one cow that speaks Russian, Ma's-Cow.

ORANGE STUFFED SQUASH

Orange flavored with crunchy pecans on top. Delicious variation.

Acorn squash	**3**	**3**
Squash pulp		
Brown sugar, packed	**⅓ cup**	**75 mL**
Butter or margarine, softened	**3 tbsp.**	**45 mL**
Grated orange peel	**1½ tsp.**	**7 mL**
Prepared orange juice	**⅓ cup**	**75 mL**
Salt	**1 tsp.**	**5 mL**
Chopped pecans (optional)	**2 tbsp.**	**30 mL**

Cut squash in half lengthwise. Discard seeds. Arrange cut side down in greased baking pan. Bake uncovered in 350°F (180°C) oven for about 35 minutes until tender.

Scoop out pulp leaving shells intact. Mix pulp with sugar, butter, orange peel, juice and salt. Stuff 4 shells full or 6 shells if you would rather have them partially full.

Sprinkle with pecans. Bake uncovered in 350°F (180°C) oven until heated through, about 15 minutes. Serves 4 to 6.

SUGAR PUMPKIN: Peel and cut pumpkin into large cubes. Cook in salted water. Toss with butter or margarine. Sprinkle with salt and pepper.

ONION STUFFED POTATOES

A most popular flavor.

Medium potatoes, baked	**6**	**6**
Butter or margarine	**¼ cup**	**50 mL**
Chopped onion	**1 cup**	**250 mL**
Garlic clove, minced	**1**	**1**
Potato pulp		
Sour cream	**½ cup**	**125 mL**
Salt	**1 tsp.**	**5 mL**
Pepper	**¼ tsp.**	**1 mL**

(continued on next page)

Cut ¼ inch (6 mm) slice lengthwise from potatoes. Scoop out pulp and put into bowl.

Melt butter in frying pan. Add onion and garlic. Sauté until soft and clear.

Mash potato pulp, sour cream, salt and pepper together. Add onion and butter mixture. Stir. Stuff potato shells. Arrange on baking sheet. Bake in 400°F (200°C) oven for about 15 minutes. Color may be added with a sprinkle of paprika, grated cheese or chopped green onion. Serves 6.

POTATOES AND THE WORKS

Stuffed with the most common condiments. Looks colorful.

Medium potatoes, baked	**8**	**8**
Potato pulp		
Butter or margarine, softened	**½ cup**	**125 mL**
Sour cream	**1 cup**	**250 mL**
Bacon bits	**4 tsp.**	**20 mL**
Chopped fresh chives	**4 tsp.**	**20 mL**
Grated medium Cheddar cheese	**1 cup**	**250 mL**

Cut ¼ inch (6 mm) slice lengthwise from top of each potato.

Scoop out pulp and put into bowl. Add butter and sour cream. Mash well.

Mix in bacon bits and chives. Dried chives may be used if necessary. Stuff potatoes.

Sprinkle with cheese. Place on baking sheet. Bake in 400°F (200°C) oven 15 to 20 minutes. Serves 8.

Don't carry plastic bags in your trouser pockets or you will have baggie pants.

ARTICHOKE FLORENTINE

Very flavorful using canned artichoke hearts. Seasoned bread crumbs, buttered or dry, make a good alternate topping.

Frozen chopped spinach, cooked and drained	**10 oz.**	**184 g**
Canned artichoke hearts, drained and quartered	**14 oz.**	**398 mL**
Butter or margarine	**2 tbsp.**	**30 mL**
All-purpose flour	**2 tbsp.**	**30 mL**
Salt	**½ tsp.**	**2 mL**
Pepper	**⅛ tsp.**	**0.5 mL**
Milk	**1 cup**	**225 mL**
Grated Parmesan cheese	**½ cup**	**125 mL**
Grated Parmesan cheese		

Put spinach and artichoke into 2 quart (2 L) casserole.

Melt butter in small saucepan. Mix in flour, salt and pepper. Stir in milk. Heat and stir until it boils and thickens.

Add first amount of cheese. Pour into casserole. Mix lightly with vegetables.

Sprinkle with more cheese. Bake uncovered in 350°F (180°C) oven for 25 to 30 minutes until hot. Serves 4 to 6.

Note: Sour cream may be used instead of cream sauce if desired. It is more tart.

CHOW MEIN GREEN BEANS

It takes but a few ingredients to make this.

Condensed cream of chicken soup (or celery)	**10 oz.**	**284 mL**
Green beans, any style, drained	**2 × 14 oz.**	**2 × 398 mL**
Canned chow mein noodles	**4 oz.**	**113 g**
Grated Cheddar cheese	**1½ cups**	**375 mL**

(continued on next page)

Mix soup and beans together. Turn into 2 quart (2 L) casserole.

Cover with noodles. Sprinkle cheese over all. Cover and bake in 350°F (180°C) oven for 20 minutes. Remove cover and continue to bake until cheese melts and toasts, about 10 to 15 minutes. Serves 6 to 8.

QUICK ARTICHOKE BAKE

If you have never cooked artichokes you will find this an easy and tasty way to serve them. Saucy good.

Canned artichoke hearts, drained and quartered (or use 2 × 10 oz., 2 × 284 g, frozen, cooked)	**2 × 14 oz.**	**2 × 398 mL**
Condensed cream of mushroom soup	**10 oz.**	**284 mL**
Cheese slices	**6 - 8**	**6 - 8**
Butter or margarine	**2 tbsp.**	**30 mL**
Dry bread crumbs	**½ cup**	**125 mL**

Put artichokes into 2 quart (2 L) casserole. Spoon soup over top. Cover with cheese.

Melt butter in small saucepan. Stir in bread crumbs. Sprinkle over cheese. Bake uncovered in 350°F (180°C) oven for 20 to 30 minutes until hot. Serves 8.

PINEAPPLE BEANS

Beans and pineapple, a perfect combination.

Canned baked beans	**2 × 14 oz.**	**2 × 398 mL**
Brown sugar, packed	**¼ cup**	**50 mL**
Pineapple tidbits, drained, reserve juice	**14 oz.**	**398 mL**
Prepared mustard	**1 tsp.**	**5 mL**
Salt	**¼ tsp.**	**1 mL**
Ketchup	**¼ cup**	**60 mL**

Mix all ingredients together. Put into 1½ quart (1.5 L) casserole. Bake uncovered in 350°F (180°C) oven for about 1 hour. If too dry, add a bit of reserved pineapple juice. Serves 6.

LIMA CASSEROLE

Cheesy colored with golden crumb topping. Creamy with a mild pimiento flavor.

Lima beans, drained	**14 oz.**	**398 mL**
Condensed cream of celery soup	**½ × 10 oz.**	**½ × 284 mL**
Sour cream	**¼ cup**	**50 mL**
Finely chopped onion	**¼ cup**	**50 mL**
Chopped pimiento	**1 tbsp.**	**15 mL**
Grated medium Cheddar cheese	**¼ cup**	**50 mL**
Butter or margarine	**1½ tsp.**	**7 mL**
Cracker crumbs	**¼ cup**	**50 mL**

Mix first 5 ingredients together. Put into 1 quart (1 L) casserole.

Sprinkle with cheese.

Melt butter in small saucepan. Stir in crumbs. Put over top of cheese. Bake uncovered in 350°F (180°C) oven for 35 to 45 minutes until hot and browned. Serves 3 to 4.

TOMATO BEAN CASSEROLE

The red tomato over cheese-sauced beans makes a very pretty vegetable. Saucy and good.

Butter or margarine	**¼ cup**	**60 mL**
All-purpose flour	**¼ cup**	**60 mL**
Salt	**¾ tsp.**	**4 mL**
Pepper	**⅛ tsp.**	**0.5 mL**
Prepared mustard	**½ tsp.**	**2 mL**
Paprika	**¼ tsp.**	**1 mL**
Milk	**2 cups**	**500 mL**
Shredded medium or sharp Cheddar cheese	**½ cup**	**125 mL**
Cut green beans, drained	**2 × 14 oz.**	**2 × 398 mL**
Sliced tomatoes, to cover	**2 - 3**	**2 - 3**
Salt, sprinkle		
Pepper, sprinkle		

(continued on next page)

Melt butter in saucepan. Mix in flour, salt, pepper, mustard and paprika. Stir in milk until it boils and thickens.

Add cheese. Stir to melt.

Add beans. Mix. Put into 2 quart (2 L) casserole.

Arrange tomato slices over top. Sprinkle with salt and pepper. Bake uncovered in 350°F (180°C) oven for about 30 minutes. Serves 8.

Pictured on page 125.

BROCCOLI CASSEROLE

A dandy make-ahead or even last minute. Broccoli is used from the frozen state.

Condensed cream of mushroom soup	**10 oz.**	**284 mL**
Process cheese spread	**½ cup**	**125 mL**
Frozen broccoli spears	**2 × 10 oz.**	**2 × 284 mL**
Canned French fried onion rings (or see page 79)	**3 oz.**	**79 g**

Put soup and cheese into small mixing bowl. Beat slowly to blend.

Arrange broccoli in 1½ quart (1.5 L) casserole. Pour soup mixture over top. Bake uncovered in 350°F (180°C) oven for about 45 minutes or until tender.

Spread onion rings over casserole. Return to oven and bake 10 minutes more. Serves 8.

FRESH BROCCOLI: Pick the large, bright green stalks, the ones with tightly closed green buds. Wrap in plastic and store in refrigerator a few days only.

Remove fairly thick peel from stems before cooking. You will notice a whitish green tender stock inside. Cut into strips or cut up stem and flowerettes separately. Cook in small amount of salted water until tender crisp. Drain and serve or add butter or margarine before serving. Cream Sauce (page 86) or Cheese Sauce (page 86) also enhances broccoli. Allow about 2 to 3 servings per pound (450 g) if only 1 vegetable is served.

GREEN BEAN CHESTNUT BAKE

Crunchy with a nice bit of flavor from the fried onion rings. A snap to make.

Condensed cream of mushroom soup	**10 oz.**	**284 mL**
Water chestnuts, sliced	**5 oz.**	**142 g**
Cheese slices, broken up or 1 cup (250 mL) grated Cheddar cheese	**4 × 1 oz.**	**4 × 28 g**
Hot pepper sauce	**¼ tsp.**	**1 mL**
French cut green beans, drained	**2 × 14 oz.**	**2 × 398 mL**
Canned French fried onion rings (or see page 79)	**3 oz.**	**85 g**

Heat first 4 ingredients in saucepan.

Stir in beans. Turn into 2 quart (2 L) casserole. Bake uncovered in 350°F (180°C) oven until hot, about 20 to 30 minutes.

Cover with onion rings. Bake an additional 5 minutes. This may be poured directly from saucepan into serving bowl then covered with onions. Onions may be used at room temperature right from can or heated in oven first. Serves 6 to 8.

1. Sugared Onions page 88
2. Stuffed Whole Cabbage page 110
3. Curried Corn page 80
4. Classic Carrot Ring page 105
5. Peas And Lettuce page 140

BARLEY CASSEROLE

If variety is the spice of life, this is spice. Serve instead of potatoes or rice.

Butter or margarine	**¼ cup**	**50 mL**
Chopped onion	**1 cup**	**250 mL**
Sliced fresh mushrooms	**½ cup**	**125 mL**
Barley, pearl or pot	**1 cup**	**250 mL**
Sliced almonds	**⅓ cup**	**75 mL**
Sliced green onion	**¼ cup**	**50 mL**
Salt	**¼ tsp.**	**1 mL**
Pepper	**¼ tsp.**	**1 mL**
Chicken bouillon cubes	**3 × ⅕ oz.**	**3 × 6 g**
Boiling water	**3 cups**	**750 mL**

Melt butter in frying pan. Add onion, mushrooms and barley. Sauté until lightly browned. Put into 1½ quart (1.5 L) casserole.

Add almonds, green onion, salt and pepper.

Dissolve bouillon cubes in boiling water. Add to casserole. Stir to mix. Cover. Bake in 350°F (180°C) oven for about 1½ hours until barley is tender. Serves 6 to 8.

RED BEAN BAKE

Tastes like real baked beans made from scratch.

Bacon slices	**4**	**4**
Chopped onion	**½ cup**	**125 mL**
Chili sauce	**¼ cup**	**50 mL**
Stewed tomatoes	**1 cup**	**250 mL**
Kidney beans with juice	**2 × 14 oz.**	**2 × 398 mL**

Fry bacon. Remove. Cool and crumble.

In frying pan, add onion to bacon drippings. Sauté until soft and clear.

Add chili sauce, tomatoes, beans and bacon. Stir and transfer to 2 quart (2.25 L) casserole. Bake uncovered in 350°F (180°C) oven for 1 hour. Serves 6 to 8.

THREE BEAN BAKE

A sweet and sour combination. A topping of buttered crumbs may be added to fancy it up or serve as is.

Bacon slices	**8**	**8**
Thinly sliced onion	**2 cups**	**500 mL**
Brown sugar, packed	**½ cup**	**125 mL**
Cider vinegar	**¼ cup**	**50 mL**
Salt	**½ tsp.**	**2 mL**
Pepper	**⅛ tsp.**	**0.5 mL**
Dry mustard	**½ tsp.**	**2 mL**
Baked beans in tomato sauce	**14 oz.**	**398 mL**
Kidney beans with juice	**14 oz.**	**398 mL**
Lima beans, drained	**14 oz.**	**398 mL**

Fry bacon until crisp. Crumble. Drain fat.

Cut onion in quarters lengthwise. Slice. Put into frying pan.

Add sugar, vinegar, salt, pepper and mustard. Stir. Cover and cook slowly for 20 minutes.

Mix all beans with onion and put into 2 quart (2 L) casserole. Bake uncovered in 350°F (180°C) oven for about 30 minutes. Serves 8.

RED BEAN CASSEROLE

An excellent dish. Has a sweet taste. Red beans at their best.

Bacon slices, crispy fried and crumbled	**2**	**2**
Chopped onion	**1 cup**	**250 mL**
Chopped green pepper	**⅔ cup**	**150 mL**
Chopped celery	**1 cup**	**250 mL**
Kidney beans with juice	**2 × 14 oz.**	**2 × 398 mL**
Chili sauce or ketchup	**½ cup**	**125 mL**
Brown sugar, packed	**½ cup**	**125 mL**

Combine all ingredients in 1½ quart (1.5 L) casserole. Bake uncovered in 325°F (160°C) oven for 2 hours. If it appears to be getting too dry, cover. Serves 6 to 8.

BROCCOLI RICE CASSEROLE

Top of the line. Good cheese flavor.

Frozen chopped broccoli, cooked and drained	**2 × 10 oz.**	**2 × 284 mL**
Long grain rice, cooked	**1 cup**	**250 mL**
Process cheese spread	**1 cup**	**250 mL**
Condensed cream of mushroom soup	**10 oz.**	**284 mL**
Condensed cream of chicken soup	**10 oz.**	**284 mL**
Butter or margarine	**2 tbsp.**	**30 mL**
Chopped onion	**1 cup**	**250 mL**
Butter or margarine	**2 tbsp.**	**30 mL**
Dry bread crumbs	**½ cup**	**125 mL**

Combine broccoli and rice in large container.

Mix cheese spread, mushroom soup and chicken soup together. Add to broccoli.

Put butter and onion into frying pan. Sauté until onion is soft and clear. Mix with broccoli and rice. Put into 3 quart (3 L) casserole.

Melt butter in small saucepan. Stir in crumbs. Sprinkle over top. Bake uncovered in 350°F (180°C) oven for about 30 minutes. Serves 8.

The coach gave good advice to the team. If you don't succeed at first, go on to second.

NOT SO CASUAL CARROTS

An intriguing casserole assembled in layers. Cheesy. Looks nice.

Medium carrots, peeled and sliced	**12**	**12**
Salted water		
Butter or margarine	**¼ cup**	**50 mL**
Chopped onion	**½ cup**	**125 mL**
All-purpose flour	**¼ cup**	**50 mL**
Salt	**1 tsp.**	**5 mL**
Pepper	**¼ tsp.**	**1 mL**
Celery salt	**¼ tsp.**	**1 mL**
Prepared mustard	**1 tsp.**	**5 mL**
Milk	**2 cups**	**450 mL**
Medium or sharp Cheddar cheese, sliced	**8 oz.**	**250 g**
Butter or margarine	**2 tbsp.**	**30 mL**
Dry bread crumbs	**½ cup**	**125 mL**

Cook carrots in salted water until tender. You should have 6 cups (1.3 L). Drain.

Melt first amount of butter in saucepan. Add onion and sauté until clear and soft.

Mix in flour, salt, pepper and celery salt. Stir in mustard and milk until it boils and thickens.

Layer in 2 quart (2 L) casserole as follows: ½ carrots, ½ cheese slices, ½ carrots, ½ cheese slices, all of the sauce.

Melt second amount of butter in small saucepan. Stir in crumbs. Spread over all. Bake uncovered in 350°F (180°C) oven for about 25 to 30 minutes until browned and heated through. Serves 8.

Gossip travels like a breeze which is started by a couple of wind-bags.

CELERY CRUNCH

Water chestnuts and almonds dress up this dish. It is flavored with just the right amount of Parmesan cheese.

Celery, sliced in 1 inch (2.5 cm) lengths	**4 cups**	**1 L**
Salted water		
Butter or margarine	**3 tbsp.**	**50 mL**
All-purpose flour	**3 tbsp.**	**50 mL**
Water	**1 cup**	**250 mL**
Light cream	**½ cup**	**125 mL**
Chicken bouillon powder	**1 tbsp.**	**15 mL**
Sliced mushrooms, drained	**⅓ cup**	**75 mL**
Sliced water chestnuts	**½ cup**	**125 mL**
Slivered almonds	**½ cup**	**125 mL**
Grated Parmesan cheese	**¼ cup**	**50 mL**
Butter or margarine	**3 tbsp.**	**50 mL**
Cracker crumbs	**½ cup**	**125 mL**

Cook celery in salted water until tender crisp. Drain. Place in 1½ quart (1.5 L) casserole.

Melt butter in saucepan. Mix in flour. Stir in water and cream until it boils and thickens.

Add bouillon powder, mushrooms, water chestnuts and almonds. Stir. Pour over celery.

Sprinkle with cheese.

Melt butter in small saucepan. Add cracker crumbs. Stir until mixed. Spread over all. Bake uncovered in 350°F (180°C) oven for 30 to 35 minutes until golden and celery is tender. Serves 4 to 6.

Pictured on page 107.

If angels fished would they catch holy mackerels?

BROCCOLI CHEESE CASSEROLE

Colorful and scrumptious. A good make-ahead.

Fresh broccoli, cut up	**1¼ lbs.**	**550 g**
Salted water		
Condensed cream of mushroom soup	**10 oz.**	**284 mL**
Thinly sliced celery	**1 cup**	**250 mL**
Chopped pimiento	**2 tbsp.**	**30 mL**
Grated medium or old Cheddar cheese	**½ cup**	**125 mL**
Sour cream	**½ cup**	**125 mL**
Salt	**½ tsp.**	**2 mL**
Pepper	**¼ tsp.**	**1 mL**
Butter or margarine	**1 tbsp.**	**15 mL**
Dry bread crumbs	**¼ cup**	**50 mL**

Cook broccoli in salted water until tender. Drain. Place in 1½ quart (1.5 L) casserole.

Combine next 7 ingredients and spread over top.

Melt butter in small saucepan. Stir in crumbs. Spread over top. Bake uncovered in 375°F (190°C) oven for about 25 minutes until browned and hot. Serves 6.

ZIPPY CARROTS

Quite different. The addition of horseradish adds a wee bite. Very tasty. Good make-ahead.

Sliced carrots	**3 cups**	**700 mL**
Salted water		
Mayonnaise	**½ cup**	**125 mL**
Dry onion flakes	**1 tbsp.**	**15 mL**
Prepared horseradish	**2 tbsp.**	**30 mL**
Salt	**½ tsp.**	**2 mL**
Pepper	**⅛ tsp.**	**0.5 mL**
Butter or margarine	**2 tbsp.**	**30 mL**
Dry bread crumbs	**½ cup**	**125 mL**

(continued on next page)

Cook carrots in salted water until tender. Drain. Put into 1½ quart (1.5 L) casserole.

Mix mayonnaise, onion, horseradish, salt and pepper together. Add to carrots. Stir.

Melt butter in small saucepan. Stir in crumbs. Scatter over top of casserole. Bake uncovered in 350°F (180°C) oven for 20 to 30 minutes until browned and hot. Serves 4.

CAULIFLOWER MIX

This extraordinary recipe is not just for company. It is easy to cut in half. Good mixture of vegetables.

Head of cauliflower, broken up	**2 lbs.**	**900 g**
Salted water		
Butter or margarine	**⅓ cup**	**75 mL**
All-purpose flour	**⅓ cup**	**75 mL**
Salt	**¾ tsp.**	**4 mL**
Pepper	**¼ tsp.**	**1 mL**
Milk	**2½ cups**	**600 mL**
Peas, frozen or fresh, cooked	**1 cup**	**250 mL**
Sliced mushrooms, drained	**½ cup**	**125 mL**
Grated medium Cheddar cheese	**1 cup**	**250 mL**
Grated medium Cheddar cheese	**1 cup**	**250 mL**

Cook cauliflower in salted water until barely tender. Drain.

Melt butter in saucepan. Mix in flour, salt and pepper. Stir in milk until it boils and thickens.

Add peas, mushrooms, first amount of cheese and cauliflower to sauce. Stir. This may be heated through and served now. For oven dish turn into 2 quart (2 L) casserole.

Scatter remaining cheese over top. Bake covered in 350°F (180°C) oven for about 25 minutes or until hot. Remove cover for last 10 minutes. Serves 8 to 10.

CAULIFLOWER SCALLOP

Colorful with bits of cheese and pimiento.

Large head of cauliflower, broken up, about 2 lbs. (900 g)	1	1
Salted water		
Eggs	2	2
Condensed cream of celery soup	10 oz.	284 mL
Milk	¼ cup	50 mL
Grated medium or sharp Cheddar cheese	½ cup	125 mL
Chopped pimiento (or less)	¼ cup	50 mL
Dry bread crumbs	¼ cup	50 mL
Snipped parsley	¼ cup	50 mL
Dry onion flakes	2 tsp.	10 mL
Salt	½ tsp.	2 mL
Pepper	⅛ tsp.	0.5 mL

Boil cauliflower covered in salted water for 2 minutes. Drain. Put into 2½ quart (2.5 L) casserole.

Beat eggs until frothy. Stir in remaining ingredients. Spoon over cauliflower being sure to cover all pieces. Bake uncovered in 375°F (190°C) oven for about 45 minutes. Serves 8 to 10.

Note: If using frozen cauliflower do not boil first. Also, omit milk or it will be too runny.

Pictured on page 107.

CURRIED CAULIFLOWER

Surprise your friends as well as your cauliflower with the addition of just the right amount of curry. Good choice.

Head of cauliflower, broken up	2 lbs.	1.8 kg
Salted water		
Condensed cream of chicken soup	10 oz.	284 mL
Mayonnaise	⅓ cup	75 mL
Grated medium Cheddar cheese	1 cup	250 mL
Curry powder	1 tsp.	5 mL
Butter or margarine	2 tbsp.	30 mL
Dry bread crumbs	½ cup	125 mL

(continued on next page)

Cook cauliflower in salted water until barely cooked. Drain. Put cauliflower into 2 quart (2 L) casserole.

Mix together soup, mayonnaise, cheese and curry powder. Spoon over top.

Melt butter in small saucepan. Stir in crumbs to coat. Sprinkle over top. Bake uncovered in 350°F (180°C) oven for 30 to 40 minutes. Serves 6.

CAULIFLOWER AU GRATIN

A favorite casserole, one that allows you to add cheese to suit your tastebuds.

Medium head of cauliflower, whole or broken up	**1**	**1**
Salted water		
Butter or margarine	**¼ cup**	**50 mL**
All-purpose flour	**¼ cup**	**50 mL**
Salt	**½ tsp.**	**2 mL**
Pepper	**⅛ tsp.**	**0.5 mL**
Milk	**2 cups**	**450 mL**
Grated medium or sharp Cheddar cheese	**½ cup**	**125 mL**

Cook cauliflower in salted water until barely tender. Drain. Put cauliflower into 2 quart (2 L) casserole.

Melt butter in saucepan. Mix in flour, salt and pepper. Stir in milk until it boils and thickens. Pour over cauliflower. Depending on size of cauliflower, this may be too much sauce. Add enough to cover.

Sprinkle with cheese. Bake uncovered in 375°F (190°C) oven until hot and crusty. Serves 6.

The best time to look for limes is when you're in the lime light.

CAULIFLOWER SUPREME

A real company vegetable that can be an oven dish or a top-of-the-stove dish.

Medium head of cauliflower, broken up	**1**	**1**
Salted water		
Butter or margarine	**2 tbsp.**	**30 mL**
Finely chopped onion	**⅔ cup**	**150 mL**
Chopped celery	**⅔ cup**	**150 mL**
Sliced mushrooms, drained	**10 oz.**	**284 mL**

Cook cauliflower in salted water until it is not quite done. Drain and place into 2 quart (2 L) casserole.

Melt butter in frying pan. Add onion and celery. Sauté until limp and clear. Spoon over top of cauliflower.

Scatter mushrooms over vegetables.

CHEESE SAUCE

Butter or margarine	**¼ cup**	**50 mL**
All-purpose flour	**¼ cup**	**50 mL**
Salt	**½ tsp.**	**2 mL**
Pepper	**⅛ tsp.**	**0.5 mL**
Milk	**2 cups**	**450 mL**
Process cheese spread	**½ cup**	**125 mL**

Melt butter in saucepan. Mix in flour, salt and pepper.

Stir in milk until it boils and thickens. Add cheese. Stir to melt. Pour over vegetables. May be covered and chilled until needed. About 1 hour before serving, place in 350°F (180°C) oven for about 30 minutes or more until heated through. A cover may be used or not. If not, a "top" forms which may be left or stirred in. Serves 6.

If you have a crazy rabbit and a counterfeit ten dollar bill you have a mad bunny and bad money.

SOUR CREAM CAULIFLOWER

Soup from the shelf and sour cream make this tasty, quick sauce.

Medium head of cauliflower, broken up	**1**	**1**
Salted water		
Condensed cream of onion soup	**10 oz.**	**284 mL**
Sour cream	**1 cup**	**250 mL**
Butter or margarine	**¼ cup**	**60 mL**
Herb seasoned bread crumbs	**1 cup**	**250 mL**

Cook cauliflower in salted water until tender. Drain. Put into shallow 1½ quart (1.5 L) casserole.

Mix soup with sour cream. Spoon over cauliflower.

Melt butter in small saucepan. Stir in crumbs. Spread over top. Bake uncovered in 350°F (180°C) oven for about 20 minutes until browned and bubbly hot. Serves 6.

PEROGY LAZY BOY

This is a terrific side dish.

Lasagne noodles	**10**	**10**
Mashed potato (about 12 medium)	**6 cups**	**1.35 L**
Grated medium Cheddar cheese	**3 cups**	**700 mL**
Salt	**1 tsp.**	**5 mL**
Butter or margarine	**1¼ cups**	**300 mL**
Chopped onion	**2 cups**	**500 mL**

Cook noodles as directed on package. Drain. Line bottom of greased 9 × 13 inch (22 × 33 cm) pan.

In large bowl mix mashed potato with cheese and salt. Put in layer over noodles. Put second layer of noodles over top.

Melt butter in frying pan. Add onion. Sauté until onion is clear and soft. Spoon onion and butter over noodles. Cover tightly with foil. Bake in 350°F (180°C) oven for 30 minutes. Let stand 10 minutes before cutting. Serve with sour cream. Cut into 24 pieces.

TOMATO POTATO BAKE

A colorful dish and very tasty.

Large tomatoes, peeled and sliced	**4 - 5**	**4 - 5**
Minced parsley, sprinkle		
Granulated sugar	**1 tsp.**	**5 mL**
Salt, sprinkle		
Pepper, sprinkle		
Butter or margarine	**1 tbsp.**	**15 mL**
Chopped onion	**½ cup**	**125 mL**
Mashed potato, well seasoned	**2 cups**	**500 mL**
Grated Cheddar cheese	**¼ cup**	**60 mL**

Place tomato slices into 2 quart (2 L) casserole. Sprinkle with parsley, sugar, salt and pepper.

Melt butter in small pan. Add onion. Sauté until soft but don't brown. Sprinkle over tomatoes.

Spread potato over all. If cold, pat out in round shape on waxed paper then invert over top.

Sprinkle with cheese. Bake uncovered in 350°F (180°C) oven until hot and browned, about 45 minutes. Serves 4 to 6.

Note: Small tomatoes left whole may be used, especially if you have some in the freezer.

SPINACH BAKE

The ever popular combination of cheese and spinach. This contains three kinds of cheese.

Eggs	**3**	**3**
Cottage cheese	**1½ cups**	**350 mL**
Grated Cheddar cheese	**1 cup**	**250 mL**
Grated Swiss cheese	**1 cup**	**250 mL**
Butter or margarine, melted	**¼ cup**	**50 mL**
Salt	**½ tsp.**	**2 mL**
Pepper	**⅛ tsp.**	**1 mL**
Nutmeg, a pinch		
Frozen spinach, cooked and drained well	**10 oz.**	**284 mL**

(continued on next page)

Beat eggs in bowl. Mix in cottage, Cheddar and Swiss cheese, butter, salt, pepper and nutmeg.

Add drained spinach to egg mixture. Stir. Pour into 2 quart (2 L) casserole. Cover. Bake in 350°F (180°C) oven for 45 to 55 minutes. Casserole will test done if you insert a knife and it comes out clean. Serves 8.

SPINACH: Boil spinach in salted water. Drain. Sprinkle with salt and pepper. Dab with butter or margarine.

CREAMED SPINACH: Stir cooked spinach into Cream Sauce (page 86). Add ⅛ to ¼ tsp. (0.5 to 1 mL) nutmeg. Heat through.

DANDELION GREENS: Use leaves before blossoms appear. Some grocery stores now carry these greens. Prepare the same as Spinach. A touch stronger green.

SQUASH AU GRATIN

Cheese topping is an extra benefit in flavor that goes well with squash.

Yellow squash, peeled and cut up	**2 lbs.**	**900 g**
Chopped onion	**½ cup**	**125 mL**
Granulated sugar (optional)	**1 tsp.**	**5 mL**
Salted water		
Eggs	**2**	**2**
Butter or margarine, softened	**2 tbsp.**	**30 mL**
Salt	**½ tsp.**	**2 mL**
Pepper	**⅛ tsp.**	**0.5 mL**
Paprika	**¼ tsp.**	**1 mL**
Grated medium Cheddar cheese	**1 cup**	**250 mL**

Cook squash and onion in sugar and salted water until tender. Drain and mash.

Beat eggs, butter, salt, pepper and paprika together. Add squash. Stir. Pour into 2 quart (2 L) casserole.

Sprinkle cheese over top. You may need more cheese depending on width of casserole. Cook uncovered in 350°F (180°C) oven for about 30 minutes until heated through. Serves 8.

SWISS CHARD DELUXE

Not your usual boiled greens. Try them with tomato.

Swiss chard, cut up and packed	**5 cups**	**1.1 L**
Canned tomatoes	**2 cups**	**500 mL**
Chopped onion	**¾ cup**	**175 mL**
Butter or margarine	**3 tbsp.**	**50 mL**
All-purpose flour	**2 tbsp.**	**30 mL**
Salt	**½ tsp.**	**2 mL**
Pepper	**⅛ tsp.**	**0.5 mL**
Granulated sugar	**1 tsp.**	**5 mL**
Milk	**½ cup**	**125 mL**
Dry bread crumbs	**½ cup**	**125 mL**
Butter or margarine	**2 tbsp.**	**30 mL**

Put chard, tomatoes and onion into saucepan. Avoid using too much white ribs. Simmer covered for 5 minutes.

Melt first amount of butter in saucepan. Mix in flour, salt, pepper and sugar. Stir in milk until it boils and thickens. It will be thick. Mix with chard mixture. Pour into 1½ quart (1.5 L) casserole.

Mix bread crumbs into remaining butter in small saucepan over medium heat. Sprinkle over all. Bake uncovered in 350° F (180°C) oven for about 30 minutes. Serves 6.

CHARD: Cook in salted water. If white part is very large, chop and cook longer. This works better if green and white are cooked separately. Sprinkle with salt and pepper. Dab with butter.

TURNIP CHEESE CASSEROLE

A rich flavor, this is creamy orange in color.

Mashed yellow turnip	**3 cups**	**700 mL**
Cream cheese, softened	**4 oz.**	**125 g**
Butter or margarine, softened	**¼ cup**	**50 mL**
Brown sugar	**2 tbsp.**	**30 mL**
Salt, sprinkle		
Pepper, sprinkle		
Bread crumbs	**¼ cup**	**50 mL**
Butter or margarine	**1 tbsp.**	**15 mL**

(continued on next page)

Combine turnip in bowl with cheese, first amount of butter, sugar, salt and pepper. Mash. Put into 2 quart (2 L) casserole.

Stir bread crumbs into butter over medium heat in small saucepan. Scatter over top. Bake uncovered in 350°F (180°C) oven for 15 to 20 minutes until hot. Serves 6 to 8.

CABBAGE AU GRATIN

A number of variations here. As well as a cheese covering, buttered crumbs can always be sprinkled over all for a final topping. Excellent.

Medium cabbage, chopped	**1½ lbs.**	**700 g**
Small onion, chopped	**1**	**1**
Salted water		
Butter or margarine	**3 tbsp.**	**50 mL**
All-purpose flour	**3 tbsp.**	**50 mL**
Salt	**½ tsp.**	**2 mL**
Pepper	**⅛ tsp.**	**0.5 mL**
Milk	**1¾ cups**	**400 mL**
Grated Cheddar cheese (optional)	**1 cup**	**250 mL**
Grated Cheddar cheese	**1½ cups**	**375 mL**

Cook cabbage and onion in salted water until tender crisp. Drain well. Transfer into 1½ quart (1.5 L) casserole.

Melt butter in saucepan. Mix in flour, salt and pepper. Stir in milk until it boils and thickens. This is very good as is but if you prefer a cheese sauce, stir in first amount of cheese to melt. Pour over cabbage.

Sprinkle with remaining cheese. Bake uncovered in 350°F (180°C) oven for 20 to 30 minutes until hot. Serves 6.

SCALLOPED CABBAGE: Simply omit cheese. Bake with or without buttered crumbs on top.

BOILED CABBAGE: Cook cabbage with or without onion in salted water. Drain. Toss with butter or margarine and salt and pepper.

ZUCCHINI CARROT CASSEROLE

Tiny crunchy bits of carrot throughout this herb-seasoned dish.

Butter or margarine	**½ cup**	**125 mL**
Zucchini, 7 inches (18 cm) long	**4**	**4**
Grated carrot	**1 cup**	**250 mL**
Chopped onion	**1 cup**	**250 mL**
Condensed cream of mushroom soup	**10 oz.**	**284 mL**
Light cream, or milk	**½ cup**	**125 mL**
Instant chicken bouillon powder	**1 tsp.**	**5 mL**
Prepared bread stuffing crumbs	**1 cup**	**250 mL**
Salt	**¼ tsp.**	**1 mL**
Butter or margarine	**2 tbsp.**	**30 mL**
Prepared bread stuffing crumbs	**½ cup**	**125 mL**

Melt first amount of butter in frying pan. Slice unpeeled zucchini ¼ inch (6 mm) thick. Sauté zucchini slices, carrot and onion until tender. This will need to be done in batches. Add more butter if necessary.

Stir in soup, cream, bouillon powder, first amount of crumbs and salt. Transfer to 2 quart (2 L) baking dish.

Melt remaining butter in small saucepan. Stir in remaining crumbs. Scatter over top. Bake uncovered in 350°F (180°C) for about 25 minutes. Serves 8.

1. Eggplant Parmigiana page 59
2. Tomato Bean Bake page 63
3. Peas In Toast Cups page 114
4. Chili Corn Bake page 61

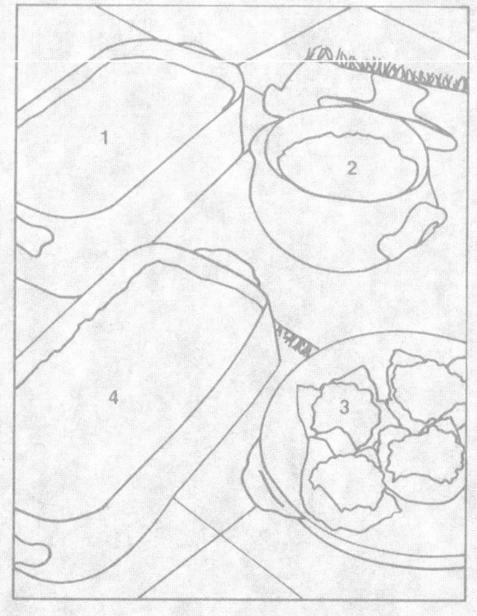

CELERY SUPREME

Contains pimiento for added flavor as well as color.

Celery, cut in 1 inch (2.5 cm) lengths	**4 cups**	**900 mL**
Salted water		
Condensed cream of chicken soup	**10 oz.**	**284 mL**
Water chestnuts, sliced	**5 oz.**	**142 mL**
Chopped pimiento	**¼ cup**	**50 mL**
Butter or margarine	**2 tbsp.**	**30 mL**
Dry bread crumbs	**½ cup**	**125 mL**

Cook celery in salted water until tender crisp. Drain. Put into 1½ quart (1.5 L) casserole.

Mix soup, water chestnuts and pimiento together and spoon over top.

Melt butter in small saucepan. Mix in crumbs. Spread over top. Bake uncovered in 350°F (180°C) oven for 30 minutes or until celery is tender. Serves 4 to 6.

CARROTS AU GRATIN

Have this in the refrigerator ready to pop into the oven.

Cooked sliced carrots	**4 cups**	**1 L**
Condensed cream of chicken soup	**10 oz.**	**284 mL**
Velveeta cheese, cut up (or use another mild, soft, process cheese)	**4 oz.**	**125 g**
Dry onion flakes	**2 tsp.**	**10 mL**
Butter or margarine	**1 tbsp.**	**15 mL**
Dry bread crumbs	**¼ cup**	**50 mL**

Put carrots into 1½ quart (1.5 L) casserole.

Mix soup, cheese and onion together in small saucepan. Heat and stir until cheese melts. Pour over carrots.

Melt butter in small saucepan. Stir in crumbs. Sprinkle over top. Bake uncovered in 350°F (180°C) oven for about 20 to 30 minutes until browned and heated through. Serves 4 to 6.

LAZY CABBAGE ROLLS

No trick at all to these. Easy to make. Use canned sauerkraut or your own.

Long grain rice	**1½ cups**	**350 mL**
Water	**1½ cups**	**350 mL**
Salt	**1 tsp.**	**5 mL**
Bacon slices, chopped	**4**	**4**
Chopped onion	**½ cup**	**125 mL**
Canned sauerkraut, drained	**19 oz.**	**540 mL**

Put rice, water and salt into saucepan. Cover. Bring to a boil. Simmer for about 15 minutes until cooked and water is absorbed.

Sauté bacon and onion together in frying pan until onion is soft and clear.

Add sauerkraut. Stir. Add rice. Mix together. Turn into 2 quart (2L) casserole. Cover. Bake in 350°F (180°C) oven for about 45 minutes. Serves 6 to 8.

HOMINY

Although this resembles popcorn in appearance, hominy is not crisp. It is soft and chewy. Baking with green chilies and sour cream creates a very uncommon dish to many.

White hominy corn, drained	**14 oz.**	**398 mL**
Chopped green chilies	**4 oz.**	**114 mL**
Sour cream	**1 cup**	**250 mL**
Salt	**½ tsp.**	**2 mL**
Pepper	**⅛ tsp.**	**0.5 mL**
Grated Monterey Jack cheese (or grated Cheddar)	**1 cup**	**250 mL**

Mix first 5 ingredients together. Put into 1 quart (1 L) casserole.

Sprinkle cheese over top. Bake uncovered in 350°F (180°C) oven for 20 to 30 minutes until hot and cheese is melted. Serves 4.

CHILI HOMINY: Add 1 tsp. (5 mL) chili powder to first 5 ingredients. Adds a bit of fire and color. Makes a completely different delicious dish.

SWEET POTATO FRUIT BAKE

Serve this incredible dish to your favorite people. It may be your favorite forever. Great with poultry or pork.

Canned sweet potatoes, drained and sliced (or use fresh, cooked)	**2 × 19 oz.**	**2 × 540 mL**
Brown sugar, packed	**1 cup**	**225 mL**
Cornstarch	**1½ tbsp.**	**25 mL**
Salt	**¼ tsp.**	**1 mL**
Crushed pineapple, drained	**14 oz.**	**398 mL**
Reserved pineapple juice plus water	**¾ cup**	**175 mL**
Butter or margarine	**¼ cup**	**50 mL**
Bananas, not too ripe, thickly sliced	**2**	**2**
Tiny marshmallows, to cover		

Put half the potatoes into 2 quart (2 L) casserole.

Mix sugar, cornstarch and salt together well in saucepan.

Add pineapple, pineapple juice and butter. Bring to a boil, stirring often to thicken.

Spread banana slices over potato in casserole. Pour pineapple mixture over banana. Top with remaining potato making as smooth as possible. Bake covered in 350°F (180°C) oven for about 20 minutes or until hot.

Cover with marshmallows. Large marshmallows may be used. Cut in half before placing on top. Return to oven uncovered for about 7 minutes until lightly browned. Serve 8 to 10 lucky folks.

Pictured on page 125.

If a physician has laryngitis would he be a hoarse doctor?

CORN PUDDING

Smooth as custard. Very pleasant.

Butter or margarine	**2 tbsp.**	**30 mL**
All-purpose flour	**2 tbsp.**	**30 mL**
Granulated sugar	**3 tbsp.**	**50 mL**
Salt	**1 tsp.**	**5 mL**
Pepper	**⅛ tsp.**	**0.5 mL**
Evaporated milk	**13½ oz.**	**385 mL**
Cream style corn, smoothed in blender	**14 oz.**	**398 mL**
Eggs, beaten	**2**	**2**

Melt butter in saucepan. Mix in flour and sugar. Remove from heat. Add salt, pepper, milk and corn. Stir.

Beat eggs until frothy. Stir into corn mixture. Turn into 2 quart (2 L) casserole. Bake uncovered in 350°F (180°C) oven for about 40 minutes. Casserole will test done if you insert a knife and it comes out clean. Serves 6.

CORN SCALLOP: Add only ¾ cup (175 mL) milk to recipe. The texture is not as much like custard.

BAKED MUSHROOMS

This will remind you of stroganoff. An excellent way to serve this classic vegetable.

Fresh small mushrooms	**3 lbs.**	**1.3 kg**
Small onion, chopped	**1**	**1**
Butter or margarine	**¼ cup**	**60 mL**
Butter or margarine	**¼ cup**	**60 mL**
All-purpose flour	**½ cup**	**125 mL**
Salt	**¾ tsp.**	**3 mL**
Pepper	**⅛ tsp.**	**0.5 mL**
Garlic powder	**¼ tsp.**	**1 mL**
Chicken stock	**2½ cups**	**500 mL**
Sour cream	**1 cup**	**225 mL**
Tomato sauce or ketchup	**1 tbsp.**	**15 mL**
Sherry (optional but good)	**1 tbsp.**	**15 mL**

(continued on next page)

Sauté mushrooms and onion in first amount of butter in frying pan for about 5 minutes. This may need to be done in two batches. Add more butter if needed. Turn into 2 quart (2 L) casserole.

Put remaining butter into frying pan. Mix in flour, salt, pepper and garlic powder. Stir in chicken stock, sour cream, tomato sauce and sherry. Heat and stir until it boils and thickens. Pour over mushrooms. Cover and bake in 350°F (180°C) oven for about 30 minutes or until bubbling hot. Serves 8.

Note: If you do not have chicken stock available use 3 chicken bouillon cubes (1/5 oz., 6 g size) dissolved in 2½ cups (500 mL) boiling water.

EGGPLANT PARMIGIANA

This will remind you of lasagne. It's saucy and cheesy.

Medium eggplants, peeled and sliced ½ inch (1.25 cm) thick	**2**	**2**
Cooking oil	**⅓ cup**	**75 mL**
Salt, sprinkle		
Pepper, sprinkle		
Tomato sauce	**2 × 7½ oz.**	**2 × 213 mL**
Oregano	**¼ tsp.**	**1 mL**
Garlic powder	**¼ tsp.**	**1 mL**
Salt	**¼ tsp.**	**1 mL**
Shredded mozzarella cheese	**2 cups**	**500 mL**
Grated Parmesan cheese	**½ cup**	**125 mL**

Fry eggplant in cooking oil over medium-high heat until browned. Salt and pepper them as they cook.

Mix tomato sauce, oregano, garlic powder and salt together.

In 2 quart (2 L) casserole put in layers of ⅓ eggplant (cut to fit), ⅓ sauce, ⅓ cheeses. Repeat 2 more times. Cover. Bake in 350°F (180°C) oven for 20 to 30 minutes. Uncover and bake 10 minutes more. Serves 6.

Pictured on page 53.

ONIONS AND PEAS

These go so well together. Great flavor.

Butter or margarine	**3 tbsp.**	**50 mL**
All-purpose flour	**3 tbsp.**	**50 mL**
Salt	**½ tsp.**	**2 mL**
Pepper	**⅛ tsp.**	**0.5 mL**
Milk	**1½ cups**	**350 mL**
Canned small white onions, drained	**14 oz.**	**398 mL**
Frozen peas, cooked	**2 × 10 oz.**	**2 × 284 g**
Butter or margarine	**1 tbsp.**	**15 mL**
Dry bread crumbs	**¼ cup**	**50 mL**

Melt butter in saucepan. Mix in flour, salt and pepper. Stir in milk until it boils and thickens. Add more milk if needed.

Add onions and peas. Turn into 1½ quart (1.5 L) casserole.

Melt butter in small saucepan. Stir in crumbs. Sprinkle over top. Bake uncovered in 350°F (180°C) oven for about 25 minutes until browned and hot. For immediate serving, vegetables may be heated in cream sauce and served without putting in oven. For serving without cream sauce, add onions to peas and cook. Serves 8.

MASHED POTATO CASSEROLE

Creamy yellow with green bits showing. Really good. This may be served as soon as prepared rather than putting into casserole to heat.

Medium-large potatoes, peeled	**8**	**8**
Bay leaves	**3**	**3**
Salted water		
Condensed cream of chicken soup	**10 oz.**	**284 mL**
Sour cream	**1 cup**	**250 mL**
Butter or margarine, softened	**¼ cup**	**50 mL**
Chopped chives	**¼ cup**	**50 mL**
Grated medium Cheddar cheese	**2 cups**	**500 mL**
Crushed cornflakes	**½ cup**	**125 mL**
Butter or margarine	**2 tbsp.**	**30 mL**

(continued on next page)

Cook potatoes and bay leaves in salted water until potatoes are tender. Drain. Discard bay leaves. Mash potatoes.

Add soup, sour cream, first amount of butter, chives and cheese. Mash well. Turn into 2½ quart (2.5 L) casserole.

Put cornflakes and butter into saucepan. Heat and stir to melt butter. Sprinkle over potato mixture. Bake in 350°F (180°C) oven until browned and heated through, about 30 to 40 minutes. Serves 8.

MASHED POTATO: Cook 6 medium potatoes in salted water. Drain. Add 2 tbsp. (30 mL) butter or margarine, ⅓ cup (75 mL) hot milk and ½ tsp. (2 mL) salt. Mash well. Add pepper and more salt if desired. To make extra fluffy, use beater. Makes 6 servings.

POTATO CAKES: Shape leftover mashed potatoes into patties. Dip into flour (optional). Brown on both sides in well greased pan. Sprinkle with salt and pepper after turning. Allow 2 cups (500 mL) for 6 patties.

CHILI CORN BAKE

An unusual corn bread with the addition of cheese and chilies. Good served with a salad and cold cuts. Nippy.

Frozen corn kernels, thawed	**2 cups**	**450 mL**
Eggs	**2**	**2**
Butter or margarine	**½ cup**	**125 mL**
Monterey Jack cheese, diced or shredded	**1 cup**	**225 mL**
Corn meal	**½ cup**	**125 mL**
Canned diced green chilies	**4 oz.**	**114 mL**
Salt	**1 tsp.**	**5 mL**
Pepper	**⅛ tsp.**	**0.5 mL**

Put corn, eggs and butter into blender. Blend until smooth. Pour into medium size bowl.

Add remaining ingredients. Stir to mix. Turn into greased 8 × 8 inch (20 × 20 cm) pan. Bake uncovered in 350°F (180°C) oven until an inserted toothpick comes out clean, about 50 to 60 minutes. Best served hot. Cuts into 16 pieces.

Pictured on page 53.

SWEET POTATO CASSEROLE

This is a delectable dish bound to please. Be sure to try it soon.

Cooked, mashed sweet potatoes, about 2 lbs. (1.8 kg)	**3 cups**	**700 mL**
Granulated sugar	**½ cup**	**125 mL**
Eggs	**2**	**2**
Butter, softened	**¼ cup**	**50 mL**
Vanilla	**1 tsp.**	**5 mL**
Salt	**¼ tsp.**	**1 mL**
Butter or margarine	**¼ cup**	**50 mL**
Brown sugar, packed	**½ cup**	**125 mL**
All-purpose flour	**¼ cup**	**50 mL**
Chopped pecans	**½ cup**	**125 mL**

Mix first 6 ingredients together. Put into 2 quart (2 L) casserole.

Melt butter in small saucepan. Add brown sugar, flour and nuts. Stir well. Sprinkle over top. Bake uncovered in 350°F (180°C) oven for about 30 minutes. Serves 8.

Variation: Add ½ tsp. (2 mL) each of cinnamon and nutmeg to first 6 ingredients. Hot or cold you will think you are eating dessert. Delicious.

SAUERKRAUT TOMATOES

A crunchy topped dish, you will find that the tomatoes soften the bite of the sauerkraut.

Canned tomatoes, drained, reserve juice	**19 oz.**	**540 mL**
Salt, sprinkle		
Pepper, sprinkle		
Butter or margarine	**½ cup**	**125 mL**
Dry bread crumbs	**2 cups**	**500 mL**
Sauerkraut, drained	**19 oz.**	**540 mL**
Reserved tomato juice		
Granulated sugar	**1 tsp.**	**5 mL**

(continued on next page)

Put tomatoes into 2 quart (2 L) casserole. Sprinkle with salt and pepper.

Melt butter in small saucepan. Stir in crumbs. Spread ½ crumbs over tomatoes.

Spoon sauerkraut over top in a layer.

Mix tomato juice and sugar together. Pour over sauerkraut.

Sprinkle second ½ crumbs over all. Bake uncovered in 350°F (180°C) oven for 20 to 30 minutes until bubbling hot and browned. Serves 8 to 10.

TOMATO BEAN BAKE

These stray from the usual baked beans. They have a bit of a different, but good, flavor.

Navy beans	**2 cups**	**500 mL**
Water	**6 cups**	**1.5 L**
Small bay leaf	**1**	**1**
Chopped onion	**2 cups**	**500 mL**
Chopped celery	**1 cup**	**250 mL**
Garlic clove, minced	**1**	**1**
Canned tomatoes	**14 oz.**	**398 mL**
Sweet pickle relish	**1 tbsp.**	**15 mL**
Brown sugar, packed	**¾ cup**	**175 mL**
Prepared mustard	**2 tsp.**	**10 mL**
Salt	**1 tsp.**	**5 mL**

Put beans, water, bay leaf, onion, celery and garlic into large heavy saucepan. Bring to a boil. Cover. Simmer for about 1 hour until skins begin to burst. Soaking beans overnight will reduce simmering time to half.

Remove bay leaf and discard. Add remaining ingredients. Turn into bean pot or 2½ quart (2.5 L) casserole. Cover. Bake in 300°F (150°C) oven for 2 to 2½ hours. Serves 8 to 10.

Pictured on page 53.

ONION AND APPLE CASSEROLE

Unusual and surprisingly good.

Brown sugar, packed	**¼ cup**	**60 mL**
Milk	**3 tbsp.**	**50 mL**
Butter or margarine, melted	**3 tbsp.**	**50 mL**
Lemon juice	**2 tsp.**	**10 mL**
Salt	**¼ tsp.**	**1 mL**
Pepper	**⅛ tsp.**	**0.5 mL**
Large onions, chopped	**2**	**2**
Large cooking apples, peeled and thinly sliced	**2**	**2**

TOPPING

Dry bread crumbs	**½ cup**	**125 mL**
Grated medium Cheddar cheese	**1 cup**	**250 mL**
Sage	**1 tsp.**	**5 mL**
Melted butter	**1 tbsp.**	**15 mL**

Measure first 6 ingredients into large bowl. Mix well.

Add onion and apple. Stir together to coat. Turn into 2 quart (2L) casserole. Cover and bake in 350°F (180°C) oven for 1 hour. Remove from oven. Cover with topping or cover with grated cheese. Bake uncovered for 30 minutes more if using topping. If using cheese only, keep covered 20 minutes more and uncover for 10 minutes.

Topping: Mix all together. Sprinkle over casserole. Return to oven. Bake uncovered until browned and apples and onion are tender. Serves 6.

Pictured on page 89.

Automobiles should come with sheer hosiery so we have cars that run.

OVEN RATATOUILLE

An easy way to cook rat-a-TOO-ee. Put all in one casserole and bake it. Can be made in the morning and baked later.

Cooking oil	**¼ cup**	**50 mL**
Thinly sliced onion	**2 cups**	**500 mL**
Large eggplant, unpeeled, chopped	**1**	**1**
Crookneck squash, unpeeled, cubed, or other summer squash	**4 cups**	**900 mL**
Medium tomatoes, peeled and cut bite size	**3**	**3**
Red or green pepper, cut in strips	**1**	**1**
Ketchup	**2 tbsp.**	**30 mL**
Salt	**1 tsp.**	**5 mL**
Pepper	**¼ tsp.**	**1 mL**
Garlic powder (optional)	**¼ tsp.**	**1 mL**

Toss all together in 3 quart (3 L) casserole to coat with oil. Cover. Bake in 350°F (180°C) oven for about 1 hour until cooked. Serves 10.

Note: To peel tomatoes, dip into boiling water for about 30 seconds, then peel.

TOMATO AU GRATIN

Cheese gives this a wonderful flavor boost. Part Monteray Jack cubes may be used if desired.

Canned tomatoes, cut up	**14 oz.**	**398 mL**
Dry bread crumbs	**¼ cup**	**50 mL**
Dry onion flakes	**1 tsp.**	**5 mL**
Cheddar cheese, cubed	**1 cup**	**250 mL**
Salt	**½ tsp.**	**2 mL**
Pepper	**⅛ tsp.**	**0.5 mL**
Granulated sugar	**1 tsp.**	**5 mL**
Butter or margarine, softened	**2 tbsp.**	**30 mL**

Stir first 7 ingredients together lightly. Turn into 1 quart (1 L) casserole.

Dot with butter. Bake uncovered in 350°F (180°C) oven for about 30 minutes. Serves 4.

TURNIP DELIGHT

Mellowed with applesauce this is a good crunchy topped make-ahead.

Cooked, mashed yellow turnip	**4 cups**	**1 L**
Applesauce, drained	**1 cup**	**250 mL**
Butter or margarine, softened	**¼ cup**	**60 mL**
Brown sugar, packed	**¼ cup**	**60 mL**
Nutmeg	**1 tsp.**	**5 mL**
Salt, sprinkle		
Pepper, sprinkle		
Butter or margarine	**2 tbsp.**	**30 mL**
Finely chopped Brazil nuts	**¼ cup**	**60 mL**
Dry bread crumbs	**½ cup**	**125 mL**

In medium saucepan heat turnip and applesauce.

Add first amount of butter, sugar, nutmeg, salt and pepper. Stir and taste. Add more salt and pepper if needed. Turn into shallow casserole.

Melt second amount of butter in small saucepan. Stir in nuts and crumbs. Sprinkle over top. Bake uncovered in 350°F (180°C) oven for about 20 minutes until browned. Serves 6.

TURNIP CASSEROLE

If you have leftover mashed turnip in your freezer, this is a delicious way to use it.

Hot mashed turnip	**3 cups**	**700 mL**
Butter or margarine, softened	**3 tbsp.**	**50 mL**
Eggs	**2**	**2**
All-purpose flour	**3 tbsp.**	**50 mL**
Brown sugar	**1 tbsp.**	**15 mL**
Baking powder	**1 tsp.**	**5 mL**
Salt	**½ tsp.**	**2 mL**
Pepper	**⅛ tsp.**	**0.5 mL**
Butter or margarine	**2 tbsp.**	**30 mL**
Cracker crumbs	**½ cup**	**125 mL**

(continued on next page)

Beat turnip, first amount of butter and eggs together well.

In small bowl mix together flour, sugar, baking powder, salt and pepper. Add to turnip mixture. Taste for salt adding more if needed. Turn into 2 quart (2 L) casserole.

Melt remaining butter in small saucepan. Stir in crumbs. Sprinkle over top. Bake uncovered in 350°F (180°C) oven for about 35 to 40 minutes until browned and hot. Serves 6 to 8.

QUICK CHEEZY POTATOES

Run sauce through the blender and you have an instant potato topping.

Medium potatoes, peeled and sliced	**8**	**8**
Medium onion, quartered	**1**	**1**
Condensed cream of mushroom soup	**10 oz.**	**284 mL**
Milk	**1 cup**	**250 mL**
Salt	**½ tsp.**	**2 mL**
Pepper	**⅛ tsp.**	**0.5 mL**
Medium or sharp Cheddar cheese, cubed	**½ lb.**	**500 g**

Put sliced potatoes into 3 quart (3 L) casserole.

Put remaining ingredients into blender. Blend smooth. Pour over potato. Cover. Bake in 350°F (180°C) oven for about 1 hour 15 minutes. Serves 8.

Variation: Use Cream Sauce (page 86) instead of soup and milk. Double recipe for sauce.

All the decision makers were on hand to hear a speech from the Chairman of the bored.

BEET TOMATO BAKE

This unusual combination will look like you are having pudding for dessert instead of a vegetable. Excellent.

Canned beets, sliced or diced, drained	**14 oz.**	**398 mL**
Grated medium Cheddar cheese	**½ cup**	**125 mL**
Canned tomatoes, cut up, with juice	**14 oz.**	**398 mL**
Grated medium Cheddar cheese	**¼ cup**	**50 mL**
Salt	**½ tsp.**	**2 mL**
Butter or margarine	**2 tbsp.**	**30 mL**
Dry bread crumbs	**½ cup**	**125 mL**

Layer first 4 ingredients in order given into 1½ quart (1.5 L) casserole. Sprinkle with salt.

Melt butter in small saucepan. Stir in crumbs. Spread over top. Bake uncovered in 350°F (180°C) oven for about 20 to 30 minutes until bubbly hot. Serves 6 to 8.

OVEN HASH BROWNS

Make this ahead of time and pop it into the oven when needed. Lots of crunchy topping. Excellent.

Frozen hash browns, thawed	**8 cups**	**1.8 L**
Chopped onion	**½ cup**	**125 mL**
Condensed cream of chicken soup	**10 oz.**	**284 mL**
Sour cream	**2 cups**	**450 mL**
Grated medium Cheddar cheese	**2 cups**	**450 mL**
Salt	**1 tsp.**	**5 mL**
Pepper	**¼ tsp.**	**1 mL**
Crushed cornflakes	**2 cups**	**500 mL**
Butter or margarine, melted	**½ cup**	**125 mL**

Mix first 7 ingredients together. Pack into 9 × 13 inch (22 × 33 cm) pan.

Mix crumbs with melted butter. Spread over top. Bake uncovered in 350°F (180°C) oven for 50 to 60 minutes. Serves 8 generously.

GREEN RICE

Just put it in the oven and forget about it for an hour. The color comes from parsley. Good.

Eggs	**2**	**2**
Cooked rice	**2 cups**	**500 mL**
Grated medium Cheddar cheese	**1 cup**	**250 mL**
Chopped onion	**1 cup**	**250 mL**
Milk	**2 cups**	**500 mL**
Butter or margarine, softened	**¼ cup**	**50 mL**
Salt	**1 tsp.**	**5 mL**
Pepper	**⅛ tsp.**	**0.5 mL**
Garlic powder (optional)	**¼ tsp.**	**1 mL**
Finely snipped parsley	**½ cup**	**125 mL**

Beat eggs with spoon in large bowl. Add remaining ingredients. Mix well. Turn into 2 quart (2 L) casserole. Add from ½ to 1 cup (125 to 250 mL) parsley until as green as you like. Bake uncovered in 325°F (160°C) oven for about 1 hour. Casserole will test done if you insert a knife and it comes out clean. Serves 8.

RICE MIX-UP

A good oven dish. Flecks of broccoli show up to give a different look.

Long grain rice	**1 cup**	**250 mL**
Chopped onion	**½ cup**	**125 mL**
Chopped celery	**½ cup**	**125 mL**
Water	**2 cups**	**500 mL**
Salt	**½ tsp.**	**3 mL**
Condensed cream of mushroom soup	**10 oz.**	**284 mL**
Frozen chopped broccoli, thawed	**10 oz.**	**284 mL**
Grated medium Cheddar cheese	**1 cup**	**250 mL**

Measure first 5 ingredients into saucepan. Cook covered until tender, about 15 minutes.

Mix soup, broccoli and cheese together. Add rice mixture. Stir. Pour into 2 quart (2 L) casserole. Cover. Bake in 350°F (180°C) oven for 40 to 50 minutes. Serves 8.

DEEP-FRIED BROCCOLI

Especially good for snack time while watching television or just visiting. Batter puffs up when cooked.

Eggs	**3**	**3**
Milk	**1½ cups**	**350 mL**
Cooking oil	**2 tsp.**	**10 mL**
All-purpose flour	**2½ cups**	**625 mL**
Granulated sugar	**¼ cup**	**50 mL**
Salt	**1½ tsp.**	**7 mL**
Broccoli stalks		
Fat for deep-frying		

Whisk together eggs, milk and cooking oil.

Mix in flour, sugar and salt.

Cut broccoli flowerettes into smaller flowerettes. Peel and cut large broccoli stems into bite size pieces.

Dip broccoli into batter to coat completely. Drop into hot fat 375°F (190°C). Cook for 3 to 5 minutes until golden brown.

DEEP-FRIED CAULIFLOWER: Simply use cauliflower instead of broccoli.

1. French Fries page 75
2. Dilled Carrots page 103
3. French Fried Onion Rings page 79
4. Celery And Carrot Garnish page 103
5. Vegetable Pizza page 16
6. Porcupines page 75
7. Tortas page 79
8. Onion Fritters page 79
9. Potato Fritters page 82

DEEP-FRIED PEPPER RINGS

A colorful display. They disappear quickly. Can be made ahead and reheated.

Peppers, green, red, yellow sliced into rings	**3**	**3**
Egg	**1**	**1**
Water	**1 tbsp.**	**15 mL**
Salt	**⅛ tsp.**	**0.5 mL**
Dry bread crumbs, rolled fine	**½ cup**	**125 mL**
Fat for deep-frying		

Pat pepper rings dry with paper towels.

Beat egg, water and salt together with fork.

Dip rings into egg mixture then into bread crumbs. Lower into hot fat 375°F (190°C) and brown. Remove to drain on paper towels. These may be fried in a greased pan but they do not brown as nicely. Serves 6.

FRIED CORN

Right from the cob. A pleasant combination.

Butter or margarine	**¼ cup**	**50 mL**
Ears of corn - cut kernels off	**4**	**4**
Chopped green pepper	**¼ cup**	**50 mL**
Chopped onion	**2 tbsp.**	**30 mL**
Salt	**½ tsp.**	**2 mL**
Pepper, sprinkle		

Combine all ingredients in frying pan or saucepan. Sauté until tender, about 4 to 6 minutes. Serves 4.

CORN ON THE COB: Add cobs to enough boiling water to cover. Return water to a boil. Cook covered for about 5 minutes. Small tender cobs require less time. Overcooking toughens corn as does cooking in salted water. Serve with butter.

Pictured on page 125.

PARSNIP CAKES

Make mashed parsnip or use leftover for this versatile cooking.

Egg	**1**	**1**
Cooked mashed parsnips	**2 cups**	**450 mL**
Butter or margarine, softened	**2 tbsp.**	**30 mL**
Granulated sugar	**½ tsp.**	**2 mL**
Salt	**⅛ tsp.**	**0.5 mL**
Pepper, sprinkle		
Fine crumbs, bread, cornflake or cracker	**⅓ cup**	**75 mL**
Paprika	**½ tsp.**	**2 mL**

Beat egg with fork in bowl. Add next 5 ingredients. Mix well. Taste for salt and pepper.

Mix crumbs and paprika together.

Shape parsnip into patties or roll into logs. If too sticky or mushy, lay on crumbs as you shape, allowing some crumbs to work into patty or log to thicken a bit. Coat well. Bake in 375°F (190°C) oven until browned, or fry in well greased pan until browned. These are a better color when deep-fried. Serves 3 to 4.

Note: Parsnips may be left in strips rather than mashed, then dipped in egg, rolled in crumbs and baked, fried or deep-fried.

Pictured on page 17.

FRIED PARSNIPS

A different tasty way to prepare parsnips. Delicious.

Parsnips	**1 lb.**	**454 g**
Butter or margarine	**2 tbsp.**	**30 mL**
Salt, sprinkle		
Pepper, sprinkle		

Peel and slice parsnips crosswise. Put into frying pan along with butter. Fry until browned. Turn, adding more butter or margarine as needed. Sprinkle with salt and pepper. Continue frying until tender when poked with tip of paring knife. Spoon into serving bowl. Serves 2 to 3.

FRENCH FRIES

Kids of all ages will dive into these.

Medium potatoes, (not new) cut in sticks or slices	6	6
Cold water		
Fat for deep-frying		
Salt, sprinkle		
Pepper, sprinkle		

Soak potatoes in water for 1 hour to remove starch and avoid clumping. Drain well. Blot dry. Soaking can be omitted if preferred.

Add enough potato just to cover bottom of deep-fryer so fat temperature won't lower too much. Cook in 365°F (160°C) fat until ends show signs of turning yellow. Centers will be white and will be fairly tender when pierced with fork. Drain on paper towels. Cool. Set aside until ready to serve or freeze in single layer for 1 hour then transfer to plastic freezer container. To serve, deep-fry in 375°F (190°C) hot fat until crisp and brown, about 4 minutes. Drain on paper towels. Sprinkle with salt and pepper. To cook in oven spread on baking sheet in 425°F (210°C) oven for about 5 minutes. Pass the ketchup and vinegar. Serves 6.

Pictured on page 71.

PORCUPINES: Shred 1 medium potato. Rinse with water. Add 2 tbsp. (30 mL) all-purpose flour. Sprinkle with salt and pepper. Stir well. Drop about 2 tbsp. (30 mL) size into fat. Drain on paper towels. Sprinkle with additional salt if needed.

Pictured on page 71.

BELL PEPPERS

This pretty three colored array is a good side dish for any barbecued meat or just serve as an extra vegetable.

Cooking oil	**2 tbsp.**	**30 mL**
Peppers, green, red and yellow, cut bite size	**4**	**4**
Salt	**1 tsp.**	**5 mL**
Pepper	**¼ tsp.**	**1 mL**

Heat cooking oil in pan. Add remaining ingredients. Cover and cook slowly for about 10 minutes. Stir often. Good hot or cold. Serves 8.

SIMPLE FRIED EGGPLANT

Egg and crumb coating before frying makes these nice and crusty.

Eggplant, peeled, sliced ½ inch (1.25 cm) thick	**1**	**1**
Egg	**1**	**1**
Water	**1 tbsp.**	**15 mL**
Salt	**½ tsp.**	**2 mL**
Pepper	**⅛ tsp.**	**0.5 mL**
Dry bread crumbs	**½ cup**	**125 mL**
Parsley flakes	**½ tsp.**	**2 mL**
Basil	**¼ tsp.**	**1 mL**
Garlic powder	**⅛ tsp.**	**0.5 mL**
Butter or margarine	**2 tbsp.**	**30 mL**

Pat eggplant dry if needed.

Beat egg, water, salt and pepper together with fork.

Mix bread crumbs, parsley, basil and garlic powder together. Dip eggplant into egg mixture then into crumbs.

Fry in melted butter in frying pan. Add more butter as needed. Fry until browned and tender. Serves 3.

FRIED RICE

A good mixture that is sure to be worth the effort in assembling it all together. This is colorful and tasty even without the addition of soy sauce.

Bacon slices, cut in small pieces	**8**	**8**
Shredded or finely chopped carrot	**1 cup**	**250 mL**
Chopped onion	**½ cup**	**125 mL**
Chopped celery	**½ cup**	**125 mL**
Chopped green onion	**⅓ cup**	**75 mL**
Cooked peas	**½ cup**	**125 mL**
Cold cooked rice	**3 cups**	**700 mL**
Soy sauce	**3 tbsp.**	**45 mL**
Salt	**¼ tsp.**	**1 mL**

(continued on next page)

Put bacon, carrot, onion and celery into frying pan. Sauté until onion is soft and clear. If it appears dry, add some cooking oil, 1 tbsp. (15 mL) at a time.

Add green onion. Sauté another 1 or 2 minutes.

Add remaining ingredients. Sauté until heated through. Check for salt. If you are not using soy sauce, you may need more salt. Serves 6 to 8.

Pictured on page 143.

OVEN AND DEEP-FRIED VEGETABLES

Baking these vegetables to simulate deep-frying gives good results for those who "must not".

Fine dry bread crumbs (or cornflake crumbs)	**¾ cup**	**175 mL**
Grated Parmesan cheese	**⅓ cup**	**75 mL**
Celery salt	**¼ tsp.**	**1 mL**
Garlic salt	**¼ tsp.**	**1 mL**
Eggs	**2**	**2**
Water	**2 tbsp.**	**30 mL**
Raw cauliflower, mushrooms, broccoli, zucchini, green pepper, red pepper		
Butter or margarine, melted	**¼ cup**	**50 mL**

Mix first 4 ingredients in bowl. Cornflake crumbs give a better color.

Beat eggs and water together with fork.

Dip vegetables into egg mixture then into crumbs. Place onto greased cookie sheet. Bake in 400°F (200°C) oven for 15 to 20 minutes until tender.

Note: When deep-fried these have a little more flavor and color.

If you eat Bison in a restaurant you will get a Buffalo Bill.

FRIED CUCUMBERS

Is your cucumber crop abundant? Try serving them hot in a tangy sauce.

Butter or margarine	**¼ cup**	**50 mL**
Chopped onion	**¼ cup**	**50 mL**
Medium cucumbers, peeled and sliced	**4**	**4**
Salt	**1 tsp.**	**5 mL**
Pepper	**¼ tsp.**	**1 mL**
Vinegar	**2 tbsp.**	**30 mL**
Granulated sugar	**2 tbsp.**	**30 mL**
Sour cream	**½ cup**	**125 mL**

Melt butter in frying pan. Add onion. Sauté until soft and clear.

Add cucumbers, salt and pepper. Sauté until lightly browned. You will have to do this in bunches.

Mix remaining ingredients together and stir into cucumber mixture. Bring to boiling point. Serves 6.

FRIED TOMATOES

Whether you use ripe, green or almost ripe tomatoes, be sure to try serving these with bacon and eggs for breakfast or brunch.

Tomatoes, sliced	**4**	**4**
Egg, fork beaten	**1**	**1**
Water	**1 tbsp.**	**15 mL**
Dry bread crumbs	**½ cup**	**125 mL**
Salt	**¾ tsp.**	**4 mL**
Pepper	**⅛ tsp.**	**0.5 mL**
Thyme	**¼ tsp.**	**1 mL**

Slice tomatoes about ⅓ inch (8 mm) thick.

Combine egg with water.

Mix crumbs, salt, pepper and thyme together well. Dip tomato into egg and coat with crumbs. Fry in greased frying pan until tender and browned on both sides. Serves 8.

FRENCH FRIED ONION RINGS

A real favorite. Try the fritters too.

Beer, fizzy or flat (or use club soda)	**1½ cups**	**375 mL**
All-purpose flour	**1½ cups**	**375 mL**
Sugar	**1 tsp.**	**5 mL**
Salt	**½ tsp.**	**2 mL**
Pepper	**⅛ tsp.**	**0.5 mL**
Large onions, peeled, cut ¼ inch (6 mm) thick and separated into rings	**3**	**3**
Fat for deep-frying		

Mix first 5 ingredients together. Let stand for at least 3 hours.

Dip onion rings into batter. Drop into hot fat 375°F (190°C) and cook until light brown.

Pictured on page 71.

ONION FRITTERS: Stir about ¼ cup (60 mL) chopped onion into ½ cup (125 mL) batter. Deep-fry by the spoonful.

Pictured on page 71.

DEEP-FRIED CAULIFLOWER: Cook tender crisp, dip in batter. Deep-fry.

DEEP-FRIED BROCCOLI: Cook tender crisp, dip in batter. Deep-fry.

TORTAS

These little fried cakes will remind you of a Denver sandwich except they contain no ham.

Eggs	**6**	**6**
Green onions, sliced	**3**	**3**
Parsley flakes	**½ tsp.**	**2 mL**
Diced tomatoes	**1 cup**	**250 mL**
Chopped green pepper	**¼ cup**	**50 mL**
Salt	**½ tsp.**	**2 mL**

Beat eggs in bowl until frothy. Add remaining ingredients. Stir. Drop by spoonfuls onto hot greased pan into 3 to 4 inch patties. Turn to cook other side. Makes 11 patties.

Pictured on page 71.

CURRIED CORN

Different and delicious. If curry intimidates you, start with half the amount.

Frozen corn kernels (or fresh)	**2 cups**	**500 mL**
Butter or margarine	**2 tbsp.**	**30 mL**
Finely chopped onion	**3 tbsp.**	**50 mL**
Curry powder	**½ tsp.**	**2 mL**
Sour cream	**½ cup**	**125 mL**
Salt	**½ tsp.**	**2 mL**
Pepper	**⅛ tsp.**	**0.5 mL**

Put first 4 ingredients into saucepan. Sauté for 1 minute. Cover and simmer slowly until tender, about 8 to 10 minutes. Stir often.

Add sour cream, salt and pepper. Serves 3.

Pictured on page 35.

FRIED SAUERKRAUT

Much tastier than heating in its own juice.

Butter or margarine	**2 - 4 tbsp.**	**30 - 60 mL**
Sauerkraut, drained	**19 oz.**	**540 mL**
Salt, sprinkle		
Pepper, sprinkle		

Melt butter in frying pan. Add drained sauerkraut. Sprinkle with salt and pepper. Sauté until browned. Serves 4.

BACON KRAUT: Fry 3 slices bacon until crisp. Crumble and add.

WIENER KRAUT: Add 4 cut up wieners.

SCRATCH BEETS

Start from scratch to produce this delicious dish. Cooks in a jiffy.

Medium size fresh beets	**4**	**4**
Butter, margarine or bacon drippings	**3 tbsp.**	**50 mL**
Salt, sprinkle		
Pepper, sprinkle		

(continued on next page)

Peel raw beets. Using medium size grater, grate and place into frying pan. Add butter. Fry, stirring and turning frequently. Sprinkle with salt and pepper to taste. When tender (taste a shred or two) spoon into serving bowl. Serve hot. Makes 4 servings.

Note: Cooked beets can be diced and sautéed in the same manner.

CORN CAKES

Similar to pancakes except these use cream style corn. Good with butter, also with syrup.

Eggs	**2**	**2**
Cream style corn	**14 oz.**	**398 mL**
All-purpose flour	**½ cup**	**125 mL**
Baking powder	**½ tsp.**	**2 mL**
Salt	**½ tsp.**	**2 mL**
Pepper	**⅛ tsp.**	**0.5 mL**
Granulated sugar	**1 tsp.**	**5 mL**

Beat eggs in mixing bowl until frothy. Add remaining ingredients. Mix. Fry in greased pan, not quite as hot as for pancakes. Makes 14 corn cakes using 2 tbsp. (30 mL) of mixture per cake. Serve with butter and syrup.

BUBBLE AND SQUEAK

An old recipe from the British Isles. Cabbage bits add both to looks and chewiness.

Mashed potato	**4 cups**	**1 L**
Cooked cabbage, chopped	**4 cups**	**1 L**
Salt	**1 tsp.**	**5 mL**
Pepper	**¼ tsp.**	**1 mL**
Butter or margarine	**2 tbsp.**	**30 mL**

Mix first 4 ingredients together. Shape into patties.

Melt butter in frying pan. Brown patties on both sides. This may be browned all in 1 big patty, turned out onto plate then eased back into pan to brown other side. If you wish it may be scramble-fried. Makes 8 good size patties or 16 medium.

POTATO FRITTERS

Serve these deep-fried potatoes piping hot. Easy to make.

Hot mashed potato	**3 cups**	**700 mL**
All-purpose flour	**2 tbsp.**	**30 mL**
Butter or margarine, softened	**3 tbsp.**	**50 mL**
Granulated sugar	**1 tsp.**	**5 mL**
Salt	**¾ tsp.**	**4 mL**
Pepper	**⅛ tsp.**	**0.5 mL**
Eggs	**2**	**2**
Fat for deep-frying		

Mix first 7 ingredients together well.

Drop by spoonfuls into 375°F (190°C) hot fat to brown, about 3 to 4 minutes. Makes about 20 fritters.

Pictured on page 71.

LENTIL CAKES

Very tasty little things. It is easy to imagine you are eating meat.

Lentils	**1 cup**	**225 mL**
Water	**2 cups**	**450 mL**
Grape-nuts cereal	**1 cup**	**225 mL**
Envelope dry onion soup	**1**	**1**
Poultry seasoning	**½ tsp.**	**2 mL**
Reserved lentil liquid plus milk to equal	**¼ cup**	**50 mL**
Eggs, beaten	**2**	**2**
All-purpose flour, for coating		
Butter or margarine, for frying		

Cook lentils, covered, in water until tender, about 15 minutes. Drain, saving liquid.

Add next 5 ingredients. Mash. Let stand 30 minutes.

Shape into 18 to 20 patties. Dip into flour. Fry in well buttered frying pan, browning both sides until dark golden. Makes 18 to 20 cakes.

Note: If grape-nuts cereal is not available, use all-bran cereal, crushed a bit.

CREAMED CUCUMBERS

Cream sauce enhances the delicate flavor of cucumbers.

Cucumbers, peeled and sliced	**2**	**2**
Salted water		
Butter or margarine	**2 tbsp.**	**30 mL**
All-purpose flour	**2 tbsp.**	**30 mL**
Salt	**½ tsp.**	**2 mL**
Pepper	**⅛ tsp.**	**0.5 mL**
Paprika	**⅛ tsp.**	**0.5 mL**
Milk	**1 cup**	**225 mL**

Cook cucumber in salted water until tender, about 10 minutes. Drain.

Melt butter in saucepan. Mix in flour, salt, pepper and paprika. Stir in milk until it boils and thickens. Add cucumbers. Mix in. Serves 4.

RADISHES IN CREAM SAUCE

An unlikely place to find this vegetable is in a cream sauce served hot.

Sliced radishes, red are best	**2 cups**	**500 mL**
Salted water		
Butter or margarine	**2 tbsp.**	**30 mL**
All-purpose flour	**2 tbsp.**	**30 mL**
Salt	**½ tsp.**	**2 mL**
Pepper	**⅛ tsp.**	**0.5 mL**
Milk	**1 cup**	**250 mL**

Cook radishes slowly in hot water until tender, about 8 to 10 minutes. Drain.

Melt butter in saucepan. Mix in flour, salt and pepper. Stir in milk until it boils and thickens. Add sliced radishes. Stir and serve. Serves 4.

STIR-FRY RADISHES: Radishes may be stir-fried in butter or margarine. Add salt and pepper.

If you see Santa Claus with a tramp, simply say "Ho Ho - Hobo".

FRESH ASPARAGUS

A simple way to serve this vegetable yet one of the best.

Asparagus	**2 lbs.**	**1 kg**
Salted water		
Butter or margarine, melted	**¼ cup**	**50 mL**
Salt, sprinkle		
Pepper, sprinkle		

Snap or cut off tough ends of asparagus. Wash. Leave whole or cut into bite size diagonal pieces. Cook in salted water until tender. If you find tips cook too fast compared to ends when cooking whole, make a pillow of foil to hold tips up. Drain very well. Turn into shallow serving dish.

Drizzle butter over top. Sprinkle with salt and pepper. Makes 4 to 6 servings of about 4 to 6 spears each.

ASPARAGUS ON TOAST: Serve with Cream Sauce, below, on buttered toast.

CREAM SAUCE		
Butter or margarine	**3 tbsp.**	**50 mL**
All-purpose flour	**3 tbsp.**	**50 mL**
Salt	**½ tsp.**	**2 mL**
Pepper	**⅛ tsp.**	**0.5 mL**
Milk	**1½ cups**	**375 mL**
Chicken bouillon powder	**1 tsp.**	**5 mL**

Melt butter in saucepan. Mix in flour, salt and pepper. Stir in milk until it boils and thickens. Stir in bouillon powder. Pour over well drained asparagus. Makes 1¾ cups.

CHEESE SAUCE: Add 1 cup (250 mL) grated Cheddar cheese, ½ cup (125 mL) cheese spread or 4 cheese slices broken, to Cream Sauce above. Stir until melted.

ASPARAGUS AMANDINE: Pour Cream Sauce over drained asparagus. Add toasted slivered almonds to sauce, about ½ cup (125 mL).

HOLLANDAISE SAUCE		
Butter or margarine	**½ cup**	**125 mL**
Lemon juice	**1½ tbsp.**	**25 mL**
Salt	**⅛ tsp.**	**0.5 mL**
Egg yolks	**2**	**2**

(continued on next page)

In saucepan melt butter with lemon juice and salt over very low heat.

Beat egg yolks well with fork. Stir into melted butter mixture. Heat slowly stirring constantly for about 1 to 2 minutes. Keep warm over warm water or sauce vegetables and serve. Especially good on asparagus, artichokes, broccoli and Brussels sprouts. Makes 1 cup (225 mL).

ASPARAGUS PARMIGIANA

Sour cream	**1 cup**	**225 mL**
Grated Parmesan cheese	**½ cup**	**125 mL**
Lemon juice	**1 tsp.**	**5 mL**
Salt	**½ tsp.**	**2 mL**
Dry mustard powder	**¼ tsp.**	**1 mL**

Heat all together without boiling. Spoon over asparagus before serving. Makes 1½ cups (375 mL) sauce.

CREAM STYLE ONIONS

These onions may be served without sauce but are a hit every time with the sauce.

Medium onions, sliced	**4**	**4**
Lots of cold water		
Salted water		
Butter or margarine	**3 tbsp.**	**50 mL**
All-purpose flour	**3 tbsp.**	**50 mL**
Salt	**½ tsp.**	**2 mL**
Pepper	**⅛ tsp.**	**0.5 mL**
Milk	**1½ cups**	**350 mL**

Cut onions into quarters lengthwise. Slice into ¼ inch (6 mm) slices. Soak in cold water about ½ to 1 hour. Drain.

Cook in salted water until tender. Drain well.

Melt butter in saucepan. Mix in flour, salt and pepper. Stir in milk until it boils and thickens. Add onion. If mixture is too thick, add a bit more milk. Serves 4.

Variation: Adding ⅛ to ¼ tsp (0.5 to 1 mL) paprika gives a warm tone to the sauce.

CAULIFLOWER

A popular vegetable available all year round. Serve it whole occasionally.

Medium head of cauliflower, whole or broken up	**1**	**1**
Salted water		

Cauliflower cooked whole needs a sauce to look complete. Broken up into flowerettes and cooked, it may be served plain, with cream sauce or with cheese sauce. Add 1 to 2 tbsp. (15 to 30 mL) lemon juice while cooking to help keep cauliflower white. Cook until tender crisp. Drain. Serve with one of the following sauces.

CREAM SAUCE

Butter or margarine	**2 tbsp.**	**30 mL**
All-purpose flour	**2 tbsp.**	**30 mL**
Salt	**¼ tsp.**	**1 mL**
Pepper, light sprinkle		
Milk	**1 cup**	**250 mL**

Melt butter in saucepan. Mix in flour, salt and pepper. Add milk. Stir until it boils and thickens. Makes about 1 cup (250 mL).

CHEESE SAUCE: Add ½ cup (125 mL) grated medium or sharp Cheddar cheese. Amount may be varied. Process cheese spread may be used as well, about ¼ cup (50 mL). More salt and cheese may be added if desired.

PARSLIED SAUCE: Add 2 tbsp. (30 mL) snipped fresh parsley to Cream Sauce or use 1½ tsp. (7 mL) dried parsley flakes.

PARMESAN SAUCE: Stir ⅓ cup (75 mL) grated Parmesan cheese into Cream Sauce.

ITALIAN SAUCE: Toss with Italian dressing using amount needed to reach flavor you like.

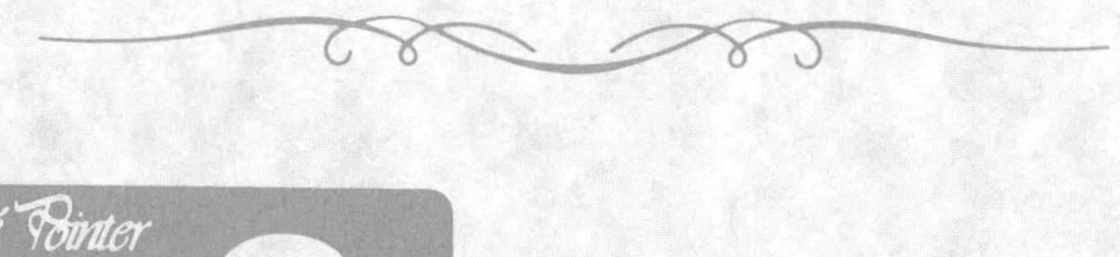

Paré Pointer

What a shock when the tom cat picked up his mail. His wife sent him a litter.

SUNSHINE SAUCE

The cheery color comes from carrots. A winning combination.

Butter or margarine	**2 tbsp.**	**30 mL**
Finely chopped onion	**¼ cup**	**50 mL**
Finely grated carrot	**½ cup**	**125 mL**
All-purpose flour	**2 tbsp.**	**30 mL**
Instant chicken bouillon powder	**1 tsp.**	**5 mL**
Water	**1 cup**	**225 mL**
Salt	**¼ tsp.**	**1 mL**

Melt butter in small saucepan. Add onion and carrot. Sauté until cooked.

Mix in flour and bouillon powder. Stir in water and salt until it boils and thickens. Serve with Classic Carrot Ring (page 105) and Peas and Lettuce (page 140) as well as other vegetables. Makes about 1 cup (225 mL).

CHEEZY DILLED PEAS

A touch of dill and a surprisingly good flavor. A cheesy sauce.

Butter or margarine	**2 tbsp.**	**30 mL**
Green onions, sliced	**2**	**2**
All-purpose flour	**2 tbsp.**	**30 mL**
Dill weed	**½ tsp.**	**2 mL**
Milk	**1¼ cups**	**300 mL**
Grated Swiss cheese	**1 cup**	**250 mL**
Salt	**¼ tsp.**	**1 mL**
Peas, fresh or frozen, cooked	**3 cups**	**700 mL**

Melt butter in saucepan. Add onion. Sauté until tender.

Mix in flour and dill weed. Stir in milk, cheese and salt until it boils and thickens and cheese is melted.

Add peas. Heat through. Serves 4.

CREAMED PEAS: Omit dill weed. Cheese is optional.

FRESH PEAS: Cook in salted water until tender. Frozen peas take 2 to 4 minutes. Fresh peas take about 15 minutes. If in doubt, taste a few.

SUGARED ONIONS

A fabulous vegetable. This would be an onion lover's dessert.

Large onions, cut in half crosswise and peeled	**4**	**4**
Salted water		
Brown sugar, packed	**⅓ cup**	**75 mL**
Vinegar	**¼ cup**	**50 mL**
Cooking oil	**2 tbsp.**	**30 mL**
Prepared mustard	**½ tsp.**	**2 mL**
Salt	**½ tsp.**	**2 mL**
Pepper	**⅛ tsp.**	**0.5 mL**

Place onions cut side up in large frying pan. Add salted water, enough to cover bottom of pan, approximately ¼ inch (6 mm) deep. Cover. Simmer 20 minutes. Add more water if needed.

Mix remaining ingredients together. Pour over onions. Continue to cook covered. Baste often. Cook until liquid is almost gone. Transfer to serving platter. Spoon any remaining sauce over top. Serves 8.

Note: If onions are strong, soak in lots of cold water ½ to 1 hour before cooking.

Pictured on page 35.

1. Onion And Apple Casserole page 64
2. Impossible Broccoli Pie page 106
3. Sour Cream Broiled Tomatoes page 20
4. Mushroom Stuffed Tomatoes page 22
5. Sesame Broiled Tomatoes page 20
6. Glazed Squash Rings page 100

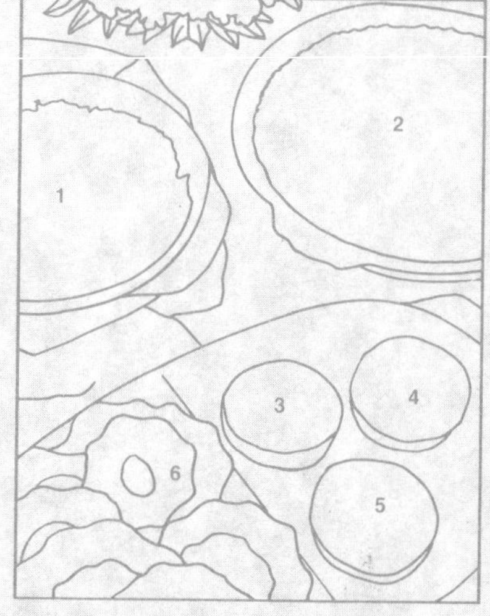

CREAMED MUSHROOMS

This delectable dish can be made at the last minute when company arrives without warning. Always a treat.

Butter or margarine	**4 tbsp.**	**60 mL**
All-purpose flour	**3 tbsp.**	**50 mL**
Salt	**¾ tsp.**	**4 mL**
Pepper	**⅛ tsp.**	**0.5 mL**
Milk	**1½ cups**	**350 mL**
Canned whole mushrooms, drained	**2 × 10 oz.**	**2 × 284 mL**

Melt butter in saucepan. Mix in flour, salt and pepper. Stir in milk until it boils and thickens.

Add mushrooms. Heat through. Serves 4.

Note: Small fresh mushrooms may be used. Simmer in sauce for about 5 minutes, stirring often.

CARROTS SUPREME

Delicious combination with onions and chicken flavor.

Medium carrots, cut in large matchsticks	**6**	**6**
Salted water		
Butter or margarine	**¼ cup**	**50 mL**
Medium onions, thinly sliced	**2**	**2**
All-purpose flour	**2 tbsp.**	**30 mL**
Water	**1 cup**	**250 mL**
Chicken bouillon powder	**2 tsp.**	**10 mL**
Granulated sugar	**½ tsp.**	**2 mL**

Cook carrots in salted water until tender. Drain.

Meanwhile, melt butter in frying pan. Add onion. Sauté until onion is soft and clear.

Mix in flour. Stir in water, bouillon powder and sugar until it boils and thickens. Add carrots. This may be kept hot or reheated in the oven. Serves 4.

ORANGE GLAZED BEETS

One of the best ways to serve this vegetable. Dazzling!

Canned beets, cut up, with juice	**14 oz.**	**398 mL**
Butter or margarine	**1 tbsp.**	**15 mL**
All-purpose flour	**2 tsp.**	**10 mL**
Brown sugar	**2 tbsp.**	**30 mL**
Salt	**⅛ tsp.**	**0.5 mL**
Prepared orange juice	**½ cup**	**125 mL**

Heat beets in saucepan.

In small saucepan melt butter. Mix in flour, sugar and salt. Stir in orange juice until it boils. Drain beets. Pour orange sauce over beets. Stir lightly. Serves 3 to 4.

Note: This makes enough sauce to cover fresh beets cooked and cut up, about 2½ cups (675 mL).

CREAMED TURNIP AND PEAS

Colorful and tasty. A different way to combine vegetables. Good choice.

Cooked diced turnip	**3 cups**	**700 mL**
Cooked peas	**1½ cups**	**375 mL**
Butter or margarine	**3 tbsp.**	**50 mL**
All-purpose flour	**3 tbsp.**	**50 mL**
Salt	**½ tsp.**	**2 mL**
Pepper	**⅛ tsp.**	**0.5 mL**
Milk	**1½ cups**	**350 mL**
Dry bread crumbs	**½ cup**	**125 mL**
Butter or margarine	**1 tbsp.**	**15 mL**

Cook turnip and peas separately. Drain. Keep hot.

Melt butter in saucepan. Mix in flour, salt and pepper. Stir in milk until it boils and thickens. Combine with diced turnip and peas. This may be served as is or put into 2 quart (2 L) casserole.

Sauté bread crumbs in second amount of butter in saucepan. Sprinkle on top of casserole and bake uncovered in 350°F (180°C) oven until bubbly hot. Serves 6 to 8.

SPICY CAULIFLOWER

Yes, ketchup on cauliflower!

Medium head of cauliflower	**1**	**1**
Salted water		
Butter or margarine	**2 tbsp.**	**30 mL**
Chopped onion	**½ cup**	**125 mL**
All-purpose flour	**2 tbsp.**	**30 mL**
Salt	**¼ tsp.**	**1 mL**
Pepper	**⅛ tsp.**	**0.5 mL**
Water	**1 cup**	**250 mL**
Ketchup	**¼ cup**	**50 mL**

Cook whole head of cauliflower in salted water. Cut into pieces if desired. Drain.

Melt butter in frying pan. Add onion. Sauté until clear and soft.

Mix in flour, salt and pepper. Stir in water and ketchup until it boils and thickens. Pour over cauliflower in bowl. Serves 6.

PURPLE OR WHITE CAULIFLOWER

Good, slightly crunchy, easy to prepare.

Medium head of cauliflower, broken up	**1**	**1**
Salted water		
Butter or margarine	**¼ cup**	**50 mL**
Fine dry bread crumbs	**3 tbsp.**	**50 mL**
Grated Parmesan cheese	**2 tbsp.**	**30 mL**

Cook cauliflower in salted water just until tender, about 8 to 10 minutes. Drain.

Brown butter in small saucepan until light brown. Be careful not to scorch. Pour over cauliflower. Toss lightly.

Stir bread crumbs and cheese together. Pour over cauliflower. Toss. Serves 6.

CANDIED SWEET POTATOES

A lemon flavor glazes these bite size pieces.

Sweet potatoes (or use 2 cans, 19 oz., 540 mL, size)	**2lbs.**	**1 kg**
Light corn syrup	**½ cup**	**125 mL**
Butter or margarine	**3 tbsp.**	**50 mL**
Lemon juice	**1 tbsp.**	**15 mL**
Grated lemon rind	**½ tsp.**	**2 mL**
Cornstarch	**1 tsp.**	**5 mL**
Water	**1 tsp.**	**5 mL**

Peel and cook potatoes. When cool enough to handle cut into bite size pieces or larger. Arrange in 2 quart (2 L) casserole.

Mix next 4 ingredients in small saucepan over medium heat.

Mix cornstarch with water. Stir into lemon mixture until it boils and thickens. Pour over potatoes. Bake uncovered in 350°F (180°C) oven for 25 to 30 minutes. Serves 8 to 10.

MASHED SWEET POTATOES: Peel, slice and cook in salted water. Drain and mash. Serve with dabs of butter or margarine and salt and pepper.

SAUCY BEANS

Tart, with a bit of a bite. This works equally well with green string beans or the wax variety.

Butter or margarine	**2 tbsp.**	**30 mL**
Finely chopped onion	**½ cup**	**125 mL**
Sour cream	**1 cup**	**250 mL**
Dill seed	**1½ tsp.**	**7 mL**
Salt	**¼ tsp.**	**1 mL**
Cut green beans or wax beans, heated and drained	**2 × 14 oz.**	**2 × 398 mL**

Melt butter in frying pan. Add onion and sauté until soft and clear.

Stir in sour cream, dill seed and salt. Simmer slowly to thicken a bit.

Put hot beans into serving dish. Spoon sauce over top. Serves 6 to 8.

MEXICAN CARROTS

Nippy and creamy, these are excellent.

Diced or sliced carrots	**3 cups**	**750 mL**
Salted water		
Cream cheese	**4 oz.**	**125 g**
Chopped green chilies	**4 oz.**	**114 mL**
Milk	**¼ cup**	**50 mL**
Salt	**½ tsp.**	**2 mL**
Pepper	**⅛ tsp.**	**0.5 mL**
Parsley sprigs for garnish		

Cook carrots in salted water until tender. Drain.

Cut in cheese. Add green chilies, milk, salt and pepper. Stir to melt and heat. Pour into serving bowl.

Garnish with parsley. Serves 4.

SAVORY CARROTS

Different and good.

Sliced carrots	**2 cups**	**500 mL**
Sliced onion	**¼ cup**	**50 mL**
Sliced celery	**¼ cup**	**50 mL**
Granulated sugar	**1 tsp.**	**5 mL**
Salt	**½ tsp.**	**2 mL**
Pepper	**¼ tsp.**	**1 mL**
Thyme	**⅛ tsp.**	**0.5 mL**
Water	**2 cups**	**500 mL**
Butter or margarine	**2 tbsp.**	**30 mL**
All-purpose flour	**2 tbsp.**	**30 mL**
Pepper	**⅛ tsp.**	**0.5 mL**
Chicken bouillon powder	**2 tsp.**	**10 mL**
Milk	**1 cup**	**250 mL**

Put first 8 ingredients into saucepan. Cook until vegetables are tender.

Melt butter in small saucepan. Mix in flour, pepper and bouillon powder. Stir in milk until it boils and thickens. Add carrots. Taste to see if more salt is needed. Serves 4.

SPECIAL SAUCED BEANS

A creamy sauce that may be halved if only a coating is desired. Exceptionally good.

Cut green beans with juice	**2 × 14 oz.**	**2 × 398 mL**
Butter or margarine	**3 tbsp.**	**50 mL**
Finely chopped onion	**¼ cup**	**60 mL**
All-purpose flour	**2 tbsp.**	**30 mL**
Milk	**1 cup**	**225 mL**
Salt, sprinkle		
Pepper, sprinkle		
Sour cream	**1 cup**	**225 mL**
Bacon slices, cooked crisp and crumbled (optional)	**4**	**4**

Heat beans in saucepan.

Meanwhile melt butter in another saucepan. Add onion. Sauté until soft. Do not brown.

Add flour to onion. Mix in. Stir in milk until it boils and thickens. Add salt and pepper to taste.

Add sour cream. Heat through without boiling. Drain beans and add to sauce. Turn into serving bowl.

Sprinkle with bacon. Serves 6 to 8.

ASPARAGUS AND PEAS

A very good combination of flavors. Quick and easy.

Canned asparagus pieces, drained	**3 × 12 oz.**	**3 × 341 mL**
Canned tiny peas, drained	**14 oz.**	**398 mL**
Butter or margarine, melted	**¼ cup**	**50 mL**
Condensed cream of mushroom soup	**2 × 10 oz.**	**2 × 284 mL**
Grated medium Cheddar cheese	**1 cup**	**250 mL**

Mix first 4 ingredients together lightly in 2 quart (2 L) casserole. Smooth top.

Sprinkle with cheese. Bake uncovered in 350°F (180°C) oven for about 30 minutes until bubbly hot. Serves 8.

SWEET AND SOUR CARROTS

One of the best variations to serve this common favorite.

Carrots, cut bite size	**2 lbs.**	**900 g**
Salted water		
Brown sugar, packed	**¼ cup**	**50 mL**
White vinegar	**¼ cup**	**50 mL**
Soy sauce	**1 tsp.**	**5 mL**
Prepared orange juice	**½ cup**	**125 mL**
Salt	**¼ tsp.**	**1 mL**
Water	**1 tbsp.**	**15 mL**
Cornstarch	**1 tbsp.**	**15 mL**

Cook carrots in salted water until tender. Drain.

While carrots are cooking put next 5 ingredients into saucepan. Mix well.

Mix water and cornstarch together. Add to saucepan. Heat and stir to boil and thicken. Pour over drained carrots. Toss lightly to coat. Serves 6 to 8.

Variation: Add ¼ cup (50 mL) chopped green pepper to carrots for the last 15 minutes of cooking.

He got fed up with doing nothing. It was too hard to stop and take a rest.

GINGERED CARROTS

For that special time this is a sure hit.

Carrots, cut bite size	**2 lbs.**	**1 kg**
Salted water		
Butter or margarine	**1 tbsp.**	**15 mL**
All-purpose flour	**2 tsp.**	**10 mL**
Brown sugar	**2 tbsp.**	**30 mL**
Ginger powder	**¼ tsp.**	**1 mL**
Prepared orange juice	**½ cup**	**125 mL**

Cook carrots in salted water until tender. Drain.

While carrots are cooking, melt butter in small saucepan. Mix in flour, sugar and ginger. Stir in orange juice until it boils and thickens slightly. Pour over drained carrots. Stir to coat. Serves 8.

CANDIED CARROTS: Simply omit ginger.

MUSTARD CARROTS

Don't be fooled by the mustard content. Flavor is surprising. Tangy but not strong. Try it. You will like it. Delicious without mustard too.

Carrots, cut up	**2 lbs.**	**900 g**
Salted water		
Butter or margarine, softened	**2 tbsp.**	**30 mL**
Brown sugar, packed	**¼ cup**	**60 mL**
Prepared mustard	**1 - 2 tbsp.**	**15 - 30 mL**
Chopped chives or parsley (optional)	**1 tbsp.**	**15 mL**
Salt, sprinkle		
Pepper, sprinkle		

Cook carrots in salted water until tender. Drain.

Mix remaining ingredients together in saucepan using smallest amount of mustard. Heat and stir to mix. Add remaining mustard until desired flavor is reached. Pour over drained carrots. Stir to coat. Serves 6 to 8.

Feed chili peppers to your pooch and have a hot dog.

GLAZED PARSNIPS

An easy method for a tasty product.

Parsnips, peeled, cut bite size	**1 lb.**	**454 g**
Salted water		
Butter or margarine	**2 tbsp.**	**30 mL**
Brown sugar	**¼ cup**	**50 mL**
Prepared orange juice	**3 tbsp.**	**50 mL**

Cook parsnips in salted water until tender. Drain.

In small saucepan bring butter, sugar and orange juice to a boil. Pour over drained parsnips. Toss lightly. Serves 3 to 4.

INSTANT GLAZED PARSNIPS: Toss parsnips with ¼ cup (50 mL) orange marmalade. Good and quick.

GREEN BEANS PARMESAN

Wax beans may be interchanged with green string beans for this simple quick dish.

Butter or margarine	**2 tbsp.**	**30 mL**
All-purpose flour	**2 tbsp.**	**30 mL**
Salt	**½ tsp.**	**2 mL**
Pepper	**⅛ tsp.**	**0.5 mL**
Milk	**1 cup**	**250 mL**
Worcestershire sauce	**½ tsp.**	**2 mL**
Grated Parmesan cheese	**2 - 4 tbsp.**	**30 - 50 mL**
Cut green beans, drained	**2 × 14 oz.**	**2 × 398 mL**

Melt butter in saucepan. Mix in flour, salt and pepper. Stir in milk until it boils and thickens. Add Worcestershire sauce and first amount of cheese. Add more to taste.

Add beans. Heat through. Stir often. Serves 8.

SAUCED GREEN BEANS: Omit Worcestershire sauce and Parmesan cheese.

FRESH BEANS PARMESAN: Cook 2 lbs. (900 g) beans in salted water. Drain. Toss with 2 tbsp. (30 mL) butter or margarine and ¼ cup (50 mL) grated Parmesan cheese. Stir well. Butter and cheese may be doubled if desired.

GLAZED SQUASH RINGS

Glistening golden rings.

Acorn squash	**2**	**2**
Hot water		
Corn syrup	**⅓ cup**	**75 mL**
Frozen concentrated orange juice	**1 tsp.**	**5 mL**

Cut squash in slices about ½ inch (12 mm) thick. Remove seeds. Arrange in 1 layer in large roaster. Add hot water about ¼ inch (6 mm) deep. Cover. Cook in 350°F (180°C) oven for 20 minutes.

Drain squash or for easy handling lift each ring to baking sheet with sides. Mix remaining ingredients together. Brush some over squash. Cook uncovered for 10 minutes. Glaze again. Cook 10 minutes. Glaze again using some from pan if necessary to cover. Cook until tender about 5 to 10 minutes. Serves 4.

Pictured on page 89.

CREAMED ONIONS AND CARROTS

A terrific combination. Good choice.

Carrots, cut in short sticks	**1 lb.**	**450 g**
Small whole white onions, peeled	**1 lb.**	**450 g**
Salted water		
Butter or margarine	**2 tbsp.**	**30 mL**
Chopped celery	**¼ cup**	**50 mL**
Condensed cream of chicken soup	**10 oz.**	**284 mL**
Sour cream	**½ cup**	**125 mL**
White wine (or apple juice)	**¼ cup**	**50 mL**
Chopped parsley	**2 tbsp.**	**30 mL**

Cook carrots and onions in salted water for about 15 minutes until tender. Drain.

Melt butter in saucepan. Add celery. Sauté until tender.

Add remaining ingredients. Mix well. Add carrot and onion. Heat through. Serves 6.

MUSHROOMS IN SOUR CREAM

Just made to serve with steak or any meat. The dill adds the extra touch. Easy to double.

Butter or margarine	**¼ cup**	**50 mL**
Chopped onion	**1 cup**	**250 mL**
Fresh mushrooms, sliced	**1 lb.**	**450 g**
Sour cream	**1 cup**	**250 mL**
Dill weed	**1 tsp.**	**5 mL**
Garlic powder	**¼ tsp.**	**1 mL**
Salt, sprinkle		
Pepper, sprinkle		

Melt butter in frying pan. Add onion. Sauté until soft and clear.

Add mushrooms. Sauté until lightly browned.

Add remaining ingredients. Stir to heat through but not to boil. Serves 4.

KOHLRABI

Bulbs with fingers that taste like a sweet young turnip.

Kohlrabi, peeled and cubed, about 4 medium	**2 lbs.**	**900 g**
Salted water		
Butter or margarine	**2 tbsp.**	**30 mL**
All-purpose flour	**2 tbsp.**	**30 mL**
Salt	**½ tsp.**	**2 mL**
Pepper	**⅛ tsp.**	**0.5 mL**
Milk	**¾ cup**	**175 mL**

Cook kohlrabi in salted water until tender. Drain.

Melt butter in saucepan. Mix in flour, salt and pepper. Stir in milk until it boils and thickens. Add kohlrabi. Serves 6.

Variation: To cooked kohlrabi add 1 tbsp. (15 mL) butter or margarine, ¼ cup (50 mL) sour cream, 1 tbsp. (15 mL) fresh chives and a sprinkle of pepper. Stir and serve.

COOL CUKES

A great pickle that you can make one day and serve the next.

Granulated sugar	2 cups	500 mL
Pickling salt	¼ cup	60 mL
Mustard seed	1 tsp.	5 mL
Celery seed	1 tsp.	5 mL
Vinegar	1 cup	250 mL
Unpeeled cucumber, thinly sliced	8 cups	1.8 mL
Sliced onion	1 cup	250 mL
Red peppers, slivered	2	2
Green peppers, slivered	2	2

Combine first 5 ingredients in large container to make vinegar mixture. Don't worry about dissolving salt. It will dissolve on its own.

Put cucumber, onion and peppers into another large container. Pour vinegar mixture over top. Chill overnight before serving. Will keep for ages in refrigerator. Makes about 2 quarts (2L).

Pictured on page 107.

GREEN BEAN MARINADE

A bit tangy and a bit sweet, this is extra easy to make and extra good to eat.

Vinegar	⅓ cup	75 mL
Granulated sugar	⅓ cup	75 mL
Cooking oil	2 tbsp.	30 mL
Cut green beans, drained	2 × 14 oz.	2 × 398 mL
Sliced onion	½ cup	125 mL
Mayonnaise	1 cup	225 mL
Bacon slices, cooked crisp and crumbled	4	4
Salt	¼ tsp.	1 mL
Vinegar	1 tsp.	5 mL
Prepared mustard	½ tsp.	2 mL

(continued on next page)

Stir vinegar, sugar and cooking oil together to dissolve sugar.

Add beans and onion. Put into bowl. Cover. Chill for 24 hours.

Mix remaining ingredients together. Drain beans and onion mixture, then add to mayonnaise sauce. Stir. Serves 8 to 10.

DILLED CARROTS

Make these tasty carrots one day to have them ready from the next day on.

Small whole carrots (or use finger-size pieces)	**1 lb.**	**450 g**
Water		
Water	**3¾ cups**	**850 mL**
Vinegar	**1¼ cups**	**275 mL**
Pickling salt	**¼ cup**	**50 mL**
Granulated sugar	**2 tbsp.**	**30 mL**
Dill weed	**2 tsp.**	**10 mL**

Cook carrots in water until barely tender crisp. Drain.

Bring remaining ingredients to a boil in saucepan to dissolve sugar. Pour over carrots in jar or other container. Chill for 1 or 2 days.

Pictured on page 71.

CELERY AND CARROT GARNISH: Cut celery and carrot sticks close to the bottom as thinly as you can. Place in cold water. Chill until ready to use. The ends will curl.

Pictured on page 71.

Mary hit Johnny on the head with a large volume of fairy tales. That's a sure way to get a book mark.

PICKLED PEPPERS

No doubt about it — these are what Peter Piper picked a peck of.

Large onion	**1**	**1**
Green peppers	**2**	**2**
Red peppers	**2**	**2**
Yellow peppers	**2**	**2**
Cider vinegar	**1 cup**	**225 mL**
Water	**⅓ cup**	**75 mL**
Granulated sugar	**1 cup**	**225 mL**
Pickling spice	**2 tsp.**	**10 mL**
Celery seed	**½ tsp.**	**2 mL**

Halve onions lengthwise then slice thinly. Cut peppers into bite size pieces. Combine with onion in jar.

Measure remaining ingredients into saucepan. Put pickling spice and celery seed into cotton bag. Bring to a boil. Boil 1 minute. Pour over onion-pepper mixture. Chill overnight. Makes about 6 cups (1.35 L).

Pictured on page 143.

CUCUMBER SALAD

Sour cream and dill weed do wonders for cucumber.

Cucumbers, peeled, sliced paper thin	**4**	**4**
Salt	**2 tbsp.**	**30 mL**
Sour cream	**1½ cups**	**350 mL**
Vinegar	**1 tbsp.**	**15 mL**
Granulated sugar	**1 tbsp.**	**15 mL**
Pepper	**½ tsp.**	**2 mL**
Dill weed	**¾ tsp.**	**4 mL**
Salt	**¼ tsp.**	**1 mL**

Slice cucumbers into bowl. These can be scored lengthwise with a fork, thus leaving the peeling on, but it is difficult to slice them thinly enough. Sprinkle with salt. Stir to mix. Chill for about 2 hours. Drain, rinse and drain well.

Mix remaining ingredients together. Add to drained cucumber. Stir to coat. Makes 4 cups (1 L).

CLASSIC CARROT RING

A pretty sight for any table. This has a cakey texture and appearance. Fill with vegetables and serve with sauce.

Butter or margarine, softened	**½ cup**	**125 mL**
Brown sugar, packed	**½ cup**	**125 mL**
Egg yolks	**2**	**2**
Lemon juice	**1 tbsp.**	**15 mL**
Grated carrot	**1½ cups**	**350 mL**
All-purpose flour	**1 cup**	**225 mL**
Baking powder	**1 tsp.**	**5 mL**
Baking soda	**½ tsp.**	**2 mL**
Salt	**½ tsp.**	**2 mL**
Pepper	**⅛ tsp.**	**0.5 mL**
Egg whites, room temperature	**2**	**2**

Cream butter and sugar together well. Beat in egg yolks one at a time. Add lemon juice.

Stir in carrot.

Mix flour, baking powder, baking soda, salt and pepper together then stir into carrot mixture.

Beat egg whites until stiff. Fold into carrot mixture. Turn into 4 cup (1 L) greased mold. Bake uncovered in 350°F (180°C) oven for 45 to 55 minutes until firm. Unmold. Fill center with Peas and Lettuce (page 140). Serve with Sunshine Sauce (page 87). Serves 6.

Pictured on page 35.

He didn't know if the tornado did any damage to his barn or not. He hadn't found it yet.

IMPOSSIBLE BROCCOLI PIE

Super easy and super good. No pre-cooking of broccoli. Pie forms its own crust as it bakes.

Frozen chopped broccoli, thawed	**10 oz.**	**284 g**
Finely chopped onion	**¼ cup**	**50 mL**
Grated medium Cheddar cheese	**1 cup**	**225 mL**
Milk	**¾ cup**	**175 mL**
Eggs	**2**	**2**
Tea biscuit mix	**½ cup**	**125 mL**
Salt	**½ tsp.**	**2 mL**
Pepper	**⅛ tsp.**	**0.5 mL**

Spread broccoli over bottom of 9 inch (23 cm) pie plate. Sprinkle with onion then with cheese.

Measure milk, eggs, biscuit mix, salt and pepper into blender. Blend until smooth. Pour over top of cheese. Bake in 400°F (200°C) oven for 25 to 35 minutes. Pie will test done if you insert a knife and it comes out clean. Cut into 6 or 8 wedges.

Pictured on page 89.

1. Celery Crunch page 41
2. Cool Cukes page 102
3. Cauliflower Scallop page 44
4. Spaghetti Squash Supreme page 150

SPANIKOPITA

Imagine you are in Greece when you sample this spinach pie.

Frozen chopped spinach	**2 × 10 oz.**	**2 × 284 mL**
Salted water		
Chopped onion	**1 cup**	**250 mL**
Butter or margarine	**2 tbsp.**	**30 mL**
Eggs	**6**	**6**
Feta cheese, cut up	**1 cup**	**225 mL**
Parsley flakes	**1 tsp.**	**5 mL**
Prepared mustard	**½ tsp.**	**2 mL**
Garlic powder	**¼ tsp.**	**1 mL**
Salt	**½ tsp.**	**2 mL**
Pepper	**⅛ tsp.**	**0.5 mL**
Oregano	**¼ tsp.**	**1 mL**
Phyllo (filo) pastry	**1 lb.**	**450 g**
Butter or margarine, melted	**¼ cup**	**50 mL**

Cook spinach in salted water. Drain well.

Sauté onion in butter until soft and clear.

Beat eggs with spoon. Add cheese, parsley, mustard, garlic powder, salt, pepper and oregano. Mix. Add spinach and onion. Stir together.

Brush 10 inch (25 cm) pie plate with butter. Layer with 8 sheets phyllo pastry, brushing each sheet with butter as you do so. Spoon spinach mixture on top. Cover with 8 more sheets of phyllo pastry, brushing each with butter. Score top sheets into wedges but do not cut right through all top sheets. Trim edge. Bake in 375°F (190°C) oven for 50 minutes. Cuts into 8 wedges.

PHYLLO TRIANGLES: Cut sheet into 3 inch (7.5 cm) widths. Brush with butter. Place 1 tsp. (5 mL) spinach filling in corner. Fold to make triangle. Keep folding to make 1 triangle. Place on greased baking sheet. Bake in 375°F (190°C) oven until browned.

Pictured on page 17.

When the chimpanzee sprained his ankle he had a monkey wrench.

STUFFED WHOLE CABBAGE

Different and picturesque, this contains meat which makes it ideal for a luncheon.

Medium-large cabbage	**2 lbs.**	**900 g**
Lean ground beef	**¾ lb.**	**350 g**
Chopped onion	**½ cup**	**125 mL**
Chopped green pepper (optional)	**2 tbsp.**	**30 mL**
Cooked long grain rice	**½ cup**	**125 mL**
Egg	**1**	**1**
Chopped cabbage	**½ cup**	**125 mL**
Salt	**1 tsp.**	**5 mL**
Pepper	**⅛ tsp.**	**0.5 mL**
Garlic powder	**⅛ tsp.**	**0.5 mL**
Canned tomatoes, mashed	**1 cup**	**250 mL**
Water	**¼ cup**	**50 mL**
Vinegar	**1½ tsp.**	**7 mL**
Granulated or brown sugar	**1½ tsp.**	**7 mL**
Oregano	**1/16 tsp.**	**0.5 mL**

Remove and save outside leaves of cabbage. Cut out core. Hollow cabbage to leave ½ inch (13 mm) shell.

Mix next 9 ingredients together in bowl. Stuff cabbage with mixture. Cover opening with outside leaves. Tie with string to hold in place. Set in small roaster, stem end down.

Mix remaining 5 ingredients together. Pour into roaster around cabbage. Cover. Bake in 325°F (160°C) oven for about 3 to 3½ hours. Cabbage should be tender when pierced. Cut into 6 wedges to serve. Spoon sauce over each wedge.

Pictured on page 35.

The harried doctor was looking through a book and without thinking he took out the section named Appendix.

ZUCCHINI QUICHE

Company zucchini at its best.

Pastry, your own or a mix, see page 113.

Butter or margarine	**¼ cup**	**50 mL**
Chopped onion	**1 cup**	**250 mL**
Unpeeled zucchini, thinly sliced	**4 cups**	**900 mL**
Chopped chives	**1 tbsp.**	**15 mL**
Parsley flakes	**1 tsp.**	**5 mL**
Salt	**½ tsp.**	**2 mL**
Pepper	**¼ tsp.**	**1 mL**
Basil	**¼ tsp.**	**1 mL**
Oregano	**¼ tsp.**	**1 mL**
Garlic powder	**¼ tsp.**	**1 mL**
Eggs	**2**	**2**
Prepared mustard	**1 tbsp.**	**15 mL**
Grated mozzarella cheese	**2 cups**	**500 mL**

Line 10 inch (25 cm) pie pan with pastry. A quiche dish may also be used. Set aside.

Melt butter in frying pan. Add onion and sauté until soft and clear. Remove onion to bowl.

Add zucchini to frying pan along with more butter if needed. Sauté for about 5 minutes being careful not to overcook it. Add to onion in bowl.

Stir in next 7 ingredients.

Beat eggs in medium bowl. Mix in mustard and cheese. Add to onion-zucchini mixture. Stir. Turn into pastry lined pan. Bake uncovered in 375°F (190°C) oven for about 20 minutes. Quiche will test done if a knife, inserted close to center, comes out clean. Serves 8.

His cough was much easier this morning which is understandable since he practiced all night.

ONION PIE

A golden crumb crust under baked onion topped with cheese.

Butter or margarine	**¼ cup**	**60 mL**
Cracker crumbs	**1 cup**	**250 mL**
Butter or margarine	**2 tbsp.**	**30 mL**
Thinly sliced onion	**2 cups**	**450 mL**
Eggs	**2**	**2**
Rich milk	**1 cup**	**225 mL**
Salt	**½ tsp.**	**2 mL**
Pepper	**⅛ tsp.**	**0.5 mL**
Grated medium Cheddar cheese	**1 cup**	**250 mL**

Melt first amount of butter in small saucepan. Stir in crumbs. Pack into 9 inch (22 cm) pie plate to form crust. Set aside.

Melt remaining butter in frying pan. Add onion. Sauté until clear but not brown. Spoon into crust.

Beat eggs. Add milk, salt and pepper. Pour over onion.

Sprinkle with cheese. Bake in 350°F (180°C) oven. Pie will test done if you insert a knife and it comes out clean. Cuts into 6 wedges.

ASPARAGUS PUFF

A soufflé-like topping covers this intriguing dish.

Canned asparagus bits, drained	**2 × 12 oz.**	**2 × 341 mL**
Butter or margarine	**3 tbsp.**	**50 mL**
All-purpose flour	**3 tbsp.**	**50 mL**
Salt	**½ tsp.**	**2 mL**
Pepper	**⅛ tsp.**	**0.5 mL**
Milk	**1 cup**	**250 mL**
Grated medium Cheddar cheese (or use Gouda or Edam)	**2 cups**	**500 mL**
Egg yolks	**4**	**4**
Egg whites	**4**	**4**

(continued on next page)

Put asparagus into 2 quart (2 L) casserole.

Melt butter in saucepan. Mix in flour, salt and pepper. Stir in milk until it boils and thickens. Remove from heat.

Stir in cheese until melted. Mix in egg yolks. Cool.

Beat egg whites until stiff. Fold into cooled sauce. Pour over asparagus. Cut a line all around top about 1 inch (2.5 cm) from outside edge. Bake uncovered in 325°F (160° C) oven for about 30 minutes. Serves 8.

Note: If using a soufflé dish, serve immediately. The collapse is not as noticeable in a casserole dish.

PIE CRUST PASTRY

Makes a tender, flaky crust for quiches, tarts and pies.

All-purpose flour	**5 cups**	**1.1 L**
Salt	**2 tsp.**	**10 mL**
Baking powder	**1 tsp.**	**5 mL**
Brown sugar	**3 tbsp.**	**45 mL**
Lard, room temperature	**1 lb.**	**454 g**
Egg	**1**	**1**
Vinegar	**2 tbsp.**	**30 mL**
Add cold water to make	**1 cup**	**225 mL**

Measure flour, salt, baking powder and brown sugar into large bowl. Stir together to distribute all ingredients.

Add lard. Cut into pieces with knife. With pastry cutter, cut in lard until whole mixture is crumbly and feels moist.

Break egg into measuring cup. Fork-beat well. Add vinegar. Add cold water to measure 1 cup (225 mL). Pour slowly over flour mixture stirring with fork to distribute. With hands, work until it will hold together. Divide into 4 equal parts. Each part is sufficient for a 2-crust pie. Use now or wrap in plastic and store in refrigerator for 1 or 2 weeks until ready to use. Store in freezer to have a continuing supply.

PEAS IN TOAST CUPS

Children of all ages adore these.

Bread slices, crust removed, buttered on both sides	**8**	**8**
Butter or margarine	**2 tbsp.**	**30 mL**
All-purpose flour	**2 tbsp.**	**30 mL**
Salt	**½ tsp.**	**2 mL**
Pepper	**⅛ tsp.**	**0.5 mL**
Milk	**1 cup**	**225 mL**
Hard-boiled eggs, cut up	**2**	**2**
Peas, cooked and drained	**1 cup**	**225 mL**

Press bread into muffin tins. Bake on bottom shelf in 350°F (180°C) oven until browned, about 15 minutes.

Melt butter in saucepan. Mix in flour, salt and pepper. Stir in milk until it boils and thickens.

Add eggs and peas. Stir. Arrange toast cups on serving plate. Spoon mixture into cups. Makes 8 small servings.

Pictured on page 53.

BROCCOLI SOUFFLÉ

Puffy and soft. A different way to serve broccoli.

Frozen chopped broccoli	**10 oz.**	**284 g**
Salted water		
Butter or margarine	**¼ cup**	**50 mL**
All-purpose flour	**¼ cup**	**50 mL**
Salt	**¼ tsp.**	**1 mL**
Pepper	**⅛ tsp.**	**0.5 mL**
Onion powder	**¼ tsp.**	**1 mL**
Grated medium Cheddar cheese	**½ cup**	**125 mL**
Milk	**½ cup**	**125 mL**
Egg whites, room temperature	**4**	**4**
Egg yolks	**4**	**4**

(continued on next page)

Cook broccoli in salted water until barely tender. Drain very well. Chop more if not already finely chopped.

Melt butter in saucepan. Mix in flour, salt, pepper, onion powder and cheese. Stir in milk until it boils and thickens. Remove from heat. Add broccoli.

Beat egg whites until stiff. Set aside.

Beat egg yolks with same beater until light and creamy. Fold into broccoli mixture.

Fold in egg whites. Turn into 2 quart (2 L) casserole. Bake uncovered in 325°F (160°C) oven, about 50 minutes. Casserole will test done if you insert a knife and it comes out clean. Serves 6.

Note: This may be baked in a soufflé dish. The collapse is more evident. It must be served immediately.

SPINACH SOUFFLÉ: Use frozen chopped spinach instead of broccoli.

RICE MUSHROOM RING

Makes a dark, shiny mold. Delicious. Will need to be doubled or tripled depending on size of ring mold.

Boiling water	**2 ⅓ cups**	**550 mL**
Beef bouillon cubes	**3 × ⅕ oz.**	**3 × 6 g**
Butter or margarine	**1 tbsp.**	**15 mL**
Box of long grain and wild rice mix	**7 oz.**	**200 g**
Butter or margarine	**¼ cup**	**50 mL**
Chopped onion	**½ cup**	**125 mL**
Chopped celery	**½ cup**	**125 mL**
Sliced mushrooms	**1 cup**	**250 mL**

Put boiling water and bouillon cubes into saucepan. Stir to dissolve. Add first amount of butter and rice. Cover. Simmer for 20 to 25 minutes. Rice should be tender and liquid should be absorbed.

Melt remaining butter in frying pan. Add onion, celery and mushrooms. Sauté until soft and add to rice. Pack into greased 4 cup (900 mL) ring mold. Can be refrigerated at this point if desired. Bake in 325°F (160°C) oven for about 20 minutes (longer if chilled). Loosen top edge if needed. Invert on plate. Serves 6.

Pictured on page 125.

LAYERED VEGETABLE LOAF

Three in one with a layer of broccoli, red studded rice and carrot.

FIRST LAYER		
Eggs	2	2
Broccoli flowerettes, cooked, drained and finely chopped	1 cup	225 mL
Butter or margarine, softened	1 tbsp.	15 mL
Grated Cheddar cheese	½ cup	125 mL
Onion salt	¼ tsp.	1 mL

SECOND LAYER		
Eggs	2	2
Cooked rice	1 cup	225 mL
Chopped red pepper	¼ cup	50 mL
Butter or margarine, softened	1 tbsp.	15 mL
Grated mozzarella cheese	½ cup	125 mL
Onion salt	¼ tsp.	1 mL

THIRD LAYER		
Eggs	2	2
Cooked mashed carrot	1 cup	225 mL
Butter or margarine, softened	1 tbsp.	15 mL
Grated Cheddar cheese	½ cup	125 mL
Onion salt	¼ tsp.	1 mL

First Layer: Spoon-beat eggs in bowl. Measure broccoli after it has been cooked and finely chopped. Add to eggs along with next 3 ingredients. Pack into well greased 8 × 4 × 2½ inch (20 × 10 × 6 mm) pan.

Second Layer: Spoon-beat second amount of eggs in bowl. Mix in next 5 ingredients. Spread over broccoli layer.

Third Layer: Spoon-beat remaining eggs in bowl. Mix in next 4 ingredients. Spread over rice layer. Bake in 325°F (160°C) oven for about 1 hour or until an inserted knife comes out clean. Unmold.

Serve with Cream Sauce (page 86). Garnish with cooked broccoli, carrot, onions and red pepper.

Pictured on cover.

He must be from the south. He always drinks from a dixie cup.

SPINACH CRÊPES

A real classic with lots of appeal. There are several steps to this recipe but the crêpes can be made well ahead.

CRÊPES		
All-purpose flour	**1 cup**	**250 mL**
Eggs	**2**	**2**
Milk	**1¼ cups**	**300 mL**
Salt	**¼ tsp**	**1 mL**
Cooking oil	**2 tbsp.**	**30 mL**
SAUCE MORNAY		
Butter or margarine	**¼ cup**	**60 mL**
All-purpose flour	**¼ cup**	**60 mL**
Salt	**¾ tsp.**	**4 mL**
Pepper	**¼ tsp.**	**1 mL**
Milk	**2 cups**	**450 mL**
Grated Swiss cheese	**¼ cup**	**60 mL**
Grated Parmesan cheese	**¼ cup**	**60 mL**
SPINACH FILLING		
Frozen chopped spinach	**10 oz.**	**284 g**
Salted water		
Portion of prepared sauce	**⅓**	**⅓**
Grated Cheddar cheese, sprinkle		

Crêpes: Measure all ingredients into small bowl. Beat until smooth. Cover and chill for about 2 hours. In greased hot crêpe pan, put 2 tbsp. (30 mL) batter. Tip pan to swirl to cover bottom of pan. More milk may be added if crêpe is too thick. When brown, crêpe may be turned and browned on other side or left only browned on 1 side. Makes about 18 to 20 crêpes.

Sauce Mornay: Melt butter in saucepan over medium heat. Mix in flour, salt and pepper. Stir in milk, Swiss and Parmesan cheese until it boils and thickens. Set aside.

Spinach Filling: Cook spinach in salted water until tender. Drain well, squeezing out moisture. Add about ⅓ of the sauce. Mix. Lay out 4 to 6 crêpes with brown sides down. Spoon spinach in a line near center. Roll. Place close together, folded side down, in pan large enough to hold a single layer. Spoon remaining sauce over top. Sprinkle with grated Cheddar cheese. Bake uncovered in 400°F (200°C) oven until hot and lightly browned. Serves 4 to 6.

ASPARAGUS CRÊPES: Lay 4 to 5 cooked asparagus spears on each crêpe. Add a spoonful of Mornay Sauce. Roll. Spoon remaining sauce over crêpes in baking pan. Sprinkle with grated Cheddar cheese. Excellent.

DEEP DARK MUSHROOMS

A delicious sauce combined with green pepper and mushrooms. These look and taste great.

Butter or margarine	**½ cup**	**125 mL**
Chopped onion	**1 cup**	**250 mL**
Fresh mushrooms, thickly cut	**1 lb.**	**450 mL**
Green pepper, cut bite size	**1**	**1**
Brown sugar, packed	**½ cup**	**125 mL**
Worcestershire sauce	**2 tsp.**	**10 mL**
Prepared mustard	**2 tsp.**	**10 mL**
Salt	**½ tsp.**	**2 mL**
Pepper	**⅛ tsp.**	**0.5 mL**

Melt butter in frying pan. Add onion. Sauté until soft.

Add mushrooms and green pepper. Sauté about 5 minutes, stirring often.

Add remaining ingredients. Stir to combine and heat. Serves 4.

MOSAIC STIR-FRY

Very colorful with three colors of peppers although one color only may be used. Good.

Cooking oil	**2 tbsp.**	**30 mL**
Sliced celery	**2 cups**	**450 mL**
Green pepper, cut in matchsticks	**⅓**	**⅓**
Red pepper, cut in matchsticks	**⅓**	**⅓**
Yellow pepper, cut in matchsticks	**⅓**	**⅓**
Large Spanish onions, sliced and separated into rings	**2**	**2**
Cider vinegar	**½ cup**	**125 mL**
Brown sugar, packed	**⅓ cup**	**75 mL**
Salt	**1 tsp.**	**5 mL**
Pepper	**¼ tsp.**	**1 mL**
Dry mustard	**½ tsp.**	**2 mL**
Water	**1½ tbsp.**	**25 mL**
Cornstarch	**1 tbsp.**	**15 mL**

(continued on next page)

Heat cooking oil in frying pan. Add next 5 ingredients. Sauté until onion is soft.

Mix vinegar, sugar, salt, pepper and mustard together. Add to vegetables. Stir.

Mix water with cornstarch. Stir into vegetables to glaze and thicken. Serves 6.

Variation: Add ½ tsp. (2 mL) caraway seeds. Simmer a bit. Excellent flavor.

STIR-FRY PEA MIXTURE

Quick and easy does it. A scrumptious dish.

Cooking oil	**1 tbsp.**	**15 mL**
Frozen Chinese pea pods (or use fresh)	**6 oz.**	**170 g**
Sliced bamboo shoots, drained	**5 oz.**	**142 g**
Sliced water chestnuts, drained	**8 oz.**	**227 mL**
Hot water	**¼ cup**	**50 mL**
Chicken bouillon powder	**1 tsp.**	**5 mL**
Soy sauce	**2 tsp.**	**10 mL**
Garlic powder	**¼ tsp.**	**1 mL**
Cornstarch	**1 tsp.**	**5 mL**
Water	**2 tsp.**	**10 mL**

Heat cooking oil in wok or frying pan. Add pea pods, bamboo shoots and water chestnuts. Stir-fry 1 minute.

Add next 4 ingredients. Stir. Cover and cook 1 minute.

Mix cornstarch and remaining water together. Stir into vegetable mixture to glaze and thicken. Serves 4.

That Russian Ox talked so much they called it Yakity-Yak.

MEATLESS CHOP SUEY

One of those dishes that doesn't call for exact quantities. Vegetables can be sautéed separately if desired and then combined.

Cooking oil	**3 tbsp.**	**50 mL**
Green pepper, cut in strips	**1**	**1**
Red pepper, cut in strips	**1**	**1**
Onions, thinly sliced	**2**	**2**
Sliced fresh mushrooms	**2 cups**	**500 mL**
Broccoli flowerettes	**2 cups**	**500 mL**
Pea pods, handful	**1**	**1**
Small suey choy, cut up (or bok choy)	**1**	**1**
Bean sprouts, handfuls	**2**	**2**
Bamboo shoots, in slivers, drained	**10 oz.**	**284 mL**
Water chestnuts, sliced, drained	**8 oz.**	**227 mL**
Water	**1 cup**	**225 mL**
Cornstarch	**1 tbsp.**	**15 mL**
Chicken bouillon powder	**1 tbsp.**	**15 mL**
Granulated sugar	**½ tsp.**	**2 mL**
Slivered almonds toasted in 350°F (180°C) oven 5 to 10 minutes until browned	**2 tbsp.**	**30 mL**

Heat cooking oil in wok. Add peppers and onion. Sauté for 2 to 3 minutes.

Add mushrooms, broccoli and pea pods. Sauté until barely tender.

Add suey choy and bean sprouts. Sauté for another minute or so.

Add bamboo shoots and water chestnuts. Heat through.

Combine water, cornstarch, bouillon powder and sugar in saucepan. Bring to a boil stirring often. Pour over vegetables. Stir lightly.

Sprinkle with almonds. Serves 8.

Pictured on page 143.

SPROUTS AND MUSHROOMS

Spruce up sprouts for a different dish.

Butter or margarine	**2 tbsp.**	**30 mL**
Sliced mushrooms	**1 cup**	**250 mL**
Chopped onion	**½ cup**	**125 mL**
Frozen Brussels sprouts	**2 × 10 oz.**	**2 × 284 mL**
Salted water		
Italian salad dressing	**⅓ cup**	**75 mL**

Put butter, mushrooms and onion into frying pan. Sauté until onion is soft and clear.

Cook Brussels sprouts in salted water until tender. Drain. Add mushroom-onion mixture to sprouts.

Add dressing. Toss to coat. Serves 6 to 8.

OKRA AND RICE

If you've never tried okra, this is a good recipe to try first. A much used vegetable in southern United States.

Butter or margarine	**2 tbsp.**	**30 mL**
Chopped onion	**1 cup**	**250 mL**
Garlic powder	**¼ tsp.**	**1 mL**
Hot pepper sauce	**½ tsp.**	**2 mL**
Salt	**¼ tsp.**	**1 mL**
Canned okra, drained	**2 × 14 oz.**	**2 × 398 mL**
Cooked rice	**1 cup**	**250 mL**

Melt butter in frying pan. Add onion, garlic powder, hot pepper sauce and salt. Sauté until onion is soft.

Add okra. Sauté to brown a bit.

Mix in rice. Heat and stir until heated through. Serves 6 to 8.

Note: Do not use iron pot as it blackens the okra.

FRESH OKRA: Slice and cook in salted water until tender. Drain. Toss with butter or margarine and salt and pepper.

STIR-FRY SPROUTS AND PEPPERS

Very colorful. Out of the ordinary.

Cooking oil	**2 tbsp.**	**30 mL**
Minced ginger root	**1 tsp.**	**5 mL**
Salt	**½ tsp.**	**2 mL**
Green pepper, cut in strips	**1**	**1**
Red pepper, cut in strips	**1**	**1**
Fresh bean sprouts	**12 oz.**	**340 g**
Chicken bouillon powder	**1 tsp.**	**5 mL**
Hot water	**¼ cup**	**50 mL**

Heat oil in wok or frying pan. Add ginger, salt and peppers. Stir-fry 2 minutes.

Add bean sprouts. Stir-fry 1 minute.

Mix bouillon powder into hot water. Add to pan. Cover. Cook 2 to 3 minutes. Serves 6.

STIR-FRY BEAN SPROUTS: Use only cooking oil and bean sprouts. Stir-fry 4 to 5 minutes. Sprinkle with salt and pepper. Serves 4.

ZUCCHINI SAUTÉ

Just like your favorite restaurant serves.

Sliced onion	**1 cup**	**250 mL**
Butter or margarine	**2 tbsp.**	**30 mL**
Sliced fresh mushrooms	**1 cup**	**250 mL**
Unpeeled zucchini, cubed	**6 cups**	**1.4 L**
Salt, sprinkle		
Pepper, sprinkle		
Garlic powder, just a touch		

Sauté onion in butter until clear and soft.

Add mushrooms. Sauté briefly. Add more butter as needed.

Add zucchini, salt, pepper and garlic powder. Sauté until heated through and barely tender. Turn into serving dish. Serves 6.

BOK CHOY STIR-FRY

A terrific mixture with a terrific flavor.

Cooking oil	**2 tbsp.**	**30 mL**
Salt	**½ tsp.**	**2 mL**
Bok choy, cut in 2 inch (5 cm) strips	**1 cup**	**250 mL**
Bean sprouts, large handful	**1**	**1**
Snow peas, large handful	**1**	**1**
Cornstarch	**1 tsp.**	**5 mL**
Chicken bouillon powder	**2 tsp.**	**10 mL**
Granulated sugar	**½ tsp.**	**2 mL**
Water	**½ cup**	**125 mL**

Heat oil in wok or frying pan. Add salt, bok choy, bean sprouts and snow peas. Stir-fry 5 to 7 minutes.

Mix cornstarch, bouillon powder and sugar together well. Add water. Stir. Add to vegetables. Stir-fry until glazed and thickened. Serves 4.

SUEY CHOY STIR-FRY: Suey Choy may be used instead of or with Bok choy.

ORIENTAL CABBAGE

The flavor is greatly improved with the addition of soy sauce.

Butter or margarine	**¼ cup**	**60 mL**
Coarsely grated cabbage	**4 cups**	**1 L**
Chopped onion	**1 cup**	**250 mL**
Chopped celery	**1 cup**	**250 mL**
Green pepper, chopped	**1**	**1**
Salt	**½ tsp.**	**2 mL**
Pepper	**⅛ tsp.**	**0.5 mL**
Soy sauce	**1 tbsp.**	**15 mL**
Paprika	**¼ tsp.**	**1 mL**

Melt butter in frying pan. Add remaining ingredients. Sauté for 2 to 3 minutes. Cover and steam 7 to 8 minutes or until tender. Check for salt to see if it needs more. Up to 2 tbsp. (30 mL) soy sauce may be added to taste. Serves 4 to 6.

VEGETABLE STIR-FRY

String beans, mushrooms and green onions sautéed in a light sauce. Tastes good.

Green beans, cut and parboiled 5 minutes	**1 cup**	**250 mL**
Sliced mushrooms	**1 cup**	**250 mL**
Green onions, sliced	**4**	**4**
Cooking oil	**1 tbsp.**	**15 mL**
Soy sauce	**1 tbsp.**	**15 mL**
Salt	**¼ tsp.**	**1 mL**
Garlic powder	**¼ tsp.**	**1 mL**
Ginger	**⅛ tsp.**	**0.5 mL**
Slivered almonds toasted in 350°F (180°C) oven 5 to 10 minutes until lightly browned	**¼ cup**	**60 mL**

Stir-fry beans, mushrooms and onion in cooking oil in wok or frying pan for 4 to 5 minutes.

Stir in remaining ingredients. Serves 3.

1. Rice Mushroom Ring page 115
2. Fried Corn page 73
3. Sweet Potato Fruit Bake page 57
4. Tomato Bean Casserole page 32

GREEN BEANS À LA FRANCE

The cooking and chilling of these beans ahead of time keeps the color fresh. They are a snap to finish at the last minute.

Green string beans, cut in short lengths	**2 lbs.**	**900 g**
Boiling water to cover		
Salt	**1 tbsp.**	**15 mL**
Butter or margarine	**6 tbsp.**	**90 mL**
Salt, sprinkle		
Pepper, sprinkle		
Lemon juice	**2 tsp.**	**10 mL**
Chopped parsley	**2 tbsp.**	**30 mL**

Cook beans in water with salt in open kettle until crunchy tender, not quite done, about 7 to 8 minutes. Bite into 1 to test. Drain. Chill by running cold water over. Keep chilled until ready to use.

Melt butter in large frying pan over medium-high heat. Add beans. Toss. Sprinkle with salt, pepper and lemon juice. Toss again until hot. Taste for salt and pepper.

Sprinkle with parsley. Serve. If serving immediately after cooking, omit the chilling. Makes 8 medium servings.

FRESH GREEN OR WAX BEANS: Green or wax beans are usually cooked in a small amount of salted water to retain vitamins. Add a splash of soy sauce for a variation.

CRUMBED BEANS

It is quick and easy to jazz up these beans right in the saucepan.

Cut green beans, drained	**14 oz.**	**398 mL**
Cracker or dry bread crumbs	**¼ cup**	**50 mL**
Butter or margarine, softened	**2 tbsp.**	**30 mL**
Salt, sprinkle		
Pepper, sprinkle		

Combine all ingredients in saucepan. Heat and toss over medium heat to coat and heat through. Serves 3 to 4.

SWEET AND SOUR BEANS

Instant flavor change. Instant approval.

Bacon slices	**4 - 6**	**4 - 6**
Chopped onion	**½ cup**	**125 mL**
All-purpose flour	**1 tbsp.**	**15 mL**
Bean juice or water	**½ cup**	**125 mL**
Salt	**½ tsp.**	**2 mL**
Pepper	**⅛ tsp.**	**0.5 mL**
White vinegar	**2 tbsp.**	**30 mL**
Granulated sugar	**1 tbsp.**	**15 mL**
Cut green beans, drained	**14 oz.**	**398 mL**

Fry bacon until crisp. Remove from pan. Cool and crumble. Set aside.

Add onion to bacon fat. Sauté until soft and clear.

Mix in flour. Stir in bean juice, salt, pepper, vinegar and sugar. Bring to a boil to thicken.

Add beans and bacon and heat through. Serves 3 to 4.

BROWNED BUTTER LIMAS

Browned butter gives this vegetable mixture a sensational flavor.

Lima beans with juice	**14 oz.**	**398 mL**
Chopped celery	**½ cup**	**125 mL**
Finely chopped onion	**½ cup**	**125 mL**
Salt	**½ tsp.**	**2 mL**
Pepper	**¼ tsp.**	**1 mL**
Beef bouillon cubes	**2 × ⅕ oz.**	**2 × 6 g**
Butter or margarine	**¼ cup**	**50 mL**

Simmer first 6 ingredients together in covered saucepan until celery and onion are tender. Drain if necessary.

In small saucepan heat butter until it browns but doesn't burn. Pour over vegetables. Vegetables will taste of too much pepper before butter is added but a great taste change takes place when tossed with butter. Serves 3 to 4.

BEETS IN JUICE

Try this to make beets beetier. Sauced with their own juice. Quick and easy.

Butter or margarine	**1 tbsp.**	**15 mL**
All-purpose flour	**1 tbsp.**	**15 mL**
Beet juice	**½ cup**	**125 mL**
Salt	**¼ tsp.**	**1 mL**
Canned beets, drained	**14 oz.**	**398 mL**

Melt butter in saucepan. Mix in flour. Stir in beet juice until it boils and thickens. Add salt.

Add beets. Simmer slowly until heated through. Serves 3.

SAVORY BRUSSELS SPROUTS

Fast preparation. The addition of thyme creates a new taste.

Frozen Brussels sprouts	**2 × 10 oz.**	**2 × 284 g**
Salted water		
Condensed cream of chicken soup	**10 oz.**	**284 mL**
Thyme	**⅛ tsp.**	**0.5 mL**
Salt, sprinkle		
Pepper, sprinkle		
Toasted almonds	**¼ cup**	**50 mL**

Cook Brussels sprouts in salted water until tender. Drain.

Into another saucepan put all remaining ingredients. Heat until barely simmering. Add drained sprouts. This may be prepared ahead and baked covered in 350°F (180°C) oven for about 30 minutes. Serves 6 to 8.

CREAMED BRUSSELS SPROUTS: Stir cooked and drained sprouts into Cream Sauce (page 86) before serving.

FRESH BRUSSELS SPROUTS: For even cooking cut an "x" in stem end. Cook in salted water until tender.

BEET GREENS

This could possibly be the best spring treat you can get.

Baby beets with tops	**1 lb.**	**450 g**
Salted water		

Choose very small beets, preferably the ones that are pulled to thin out the rows. Wash well. Push into saucepan curling tops to fit. Pour boiling water and salt over top. Cover and boil until beets are tender. Drain. Serve with butter. Serves 2 to 3.

BOILED BEETS: Choose beets all the same size, about 2 inches (5 cm) in diameter if possible. Cut off tops except for about 1 inch (2.5 cm). Wash well. Cook in salted water until tender, about 30 to 45 minutes. Drain. Peel by rubbing skin off with your fingers. Hold under cool running water to be able to handle. Return to heated pan with a very small amount of water. If using larger beets, quarter them. Toss with a dab of butter or margarine and salt and pepper them if you wish. Serves 4 to 6.

JERUSALEM ARTICHOKES

Treat this knotty tuber like a potato, not like a globe artichoke. Fun to have as an extra if you can locate them. They can be deep-fried and also eaten raw with salt and pepper.

Butter or margarine	**2 tbsp.**	**30 mL**
Jerusalem artichokes, peeled and sliced	**4**	**4**
Salt, sprinkle		
Pepper, sprinkle		

Melt butter in frying pan. Add sliced Jerusalem artichokes. Brown both sides adding more butter if needed.

Salt and pepper after turning first time. Serves 4.

BOILED JERUSALEM ARTICHOKES: Boil with or without skins in salted water until tender, about 25 minutes. Skins tend to keep pulp whiter than the usual grayish color. Can be served with butter or margarine, salt and pepper or in Cream Sauce (page 86).

HARVARD BEETS

These sweet and sour beets have a beautiful gloss to them.

Canned beets, sliced or diced	**2 × 14 oz.**	**2 × 398 mL**
Granulated sugar	**⅓ cup**	**75 mL**
Cornstarch	**3 tbsp.**	**50 mL**
Salt	**½ tsp.**	**2 mL**
Reserved beet juice	**1 cup**	**250 mL**
Vinegar	**2 tbsp.**	**30 mL**
Butter or margarine (optional)	**2 tbsp.**	**30 mL**

Drain beets. Reserve juice.

Mix sugar, cornstarch and salt together in saucepan. Stir in beet juice and vinegar. Bring to a boil. Stir until thickened.

Add butter. Stir to melt. Add beets. Heat through. Serve hot. Makes 6 to 8 servings.

GERMAN CABBAGE

Enjoy this European dish right at home.

Shredded red cabbage	**4 cups**	**1 L**
Chopped onion	**¾ cup**	**175 mL**
Cooking apples, peeled and grated	**2**	**2**
Salt	**1 tsp.**	**5 mL**
Boiling water	**½ cup**	**125 mL**
Cider vinegar	**¼ cup**	**60 mL**
Brown sugar, packed	**¼ cup**	**60 mL**
Butter or margarine, softened	**1 tbsp.**	**15 mL**
Allspice	**¼ tsp.**	**1 mL**

Measure first 5 ingredients into saucepan. Cover and cook until tender, about 10 minutes. Drain well.

Add remaining ingredients. Stir well to dissolve sugar and allspice. Serves 6.

SWEET AND SOUR BRUSSELS SPROUTS

The double flavor of sprouts and sauce make this very tasty.

Bacon slices, diced	**8**	**8**
Chopped onion	**¼ cup**	**50 mL**
Vinegar	**¼ cup**	**50 mL**
Granulated sugar	**¼ cup**	**50 mL**
Salt	**½ tsp.**	**2 mL**
Garlic powder	**¼ tsp.**	**1 mL**
Cornstarch	**2 tsp.**	**10 mL**
Water	**2 tsp.**	**10 mL**
Frozen Brussels sprouts, cooked and drained	**2 × 10 oz.**	**2 × 284 g**

Brown bacon in pan. Remove to dish.

In bacon fat, sauté onion until soft and clear.

Stir in vinegar, sugar, salt and garlic powder.

Mix cornstarch and water together. Add and stir to boil and thicken.

Add Brussels sprouts and bacon. Heat through. Serves 6 to 8.

BEETS WITH ONION

Enhance your beets with the unusual addition of onion. Really tasty.

Butter or margarine	**2 tbsp.**	**30 mL**
Sliced onion	**⅓ cup**	**75 mL**
Granulated sugar	**1 tsp.**	**5 mL**
Vinegar	**1 tsp.**	**5 mL**
Salt	**¼ tsp.**	**1 mL**
Pepper, sprinkle		
Canned beets, sliced or diced, drained	**14 oz.**	**398 mL**

Melt butter in saucepan. Add onion. Sauté until soft and clear.

Add remaining ingredients. Heat to boiling. Add a bit of beet juice or water if too dry. Serves 3 to 4.

CARROTS

These good keepers can be prepared in a multitude of ways. Only a few are listed.

Carrots, sliced or cut in sticks	**2 lbs.**	**900 g**
Salted water		
Granulated sugar	**½ tsp.**	**2 mL**
Butter or margarine, softened	**2 tbsp.**	**30 mL**
Salt, sprinkle		
Pepper, sprinkle		

Cook carrots in salted water with sugar until tender. Drain.

Add butter, salt and pepper. Toss well. Serves 8.

HOT DILLED CARROTS: Add ½ tsp. (2 mL) dill weed before tossing.

CARROTS WITH GREEN ONIONS: Cook 1 bunch green onions, sliced, with carrots. Good flavor.

CARROTS IN SAUCE: Pour Cream Sauce (page 86) over cooked carrots or warm leftover carrots in sauce.

MASHED CARROTS: Mash cooked carrots. Add butter, salt, pepper, and a bit of cream. Mash well. Different. A real hit.

CARROT BEAN DISH

Just barely creamy. Dill weed produces little green flecks throughout. The dill seed can barely be seen. Both are good.

Cooked cut green beans	**2 cups**	**500 mL**
Cooked sliced carrots	**1½ cups**	**375 mL**
Sour cream	**1 cup**	**250 mL**
Canned sliced mushrooms, drained	**½ cup**	**125 mL**
Dill seed (or dill weed)	**½ tsp.**	**2 mL**
Salt	**½ tsp.**	**2 mL**

Combine all ingredients in saucepan. Heat slowly stirring occasionally. Serves 4 to 6.

CAULIFLOWER WITH TOMATO

A colorful mixture when served with peeled and seeded tomatoes.

Medium head of cauliflower, broken up	1	1
Salted water		
Butter or margarine	1 tbsp.	15 mL
Thinly sliced onion	½ cup	125 mL
Large tomatoes, peeled, seeded and cut up	2	2
Garlic powder, light sprinkle		
Salt, sprinkle		
Pepper, sprinkle		
Chopped fresh parsley	1 tbsp.	15 mL

Cook cauliflower in salted water until tender. Drain.

Melt butter in frying pan. Add onion. Sauté until soft and clear.

Put tomatoes into boiling water for 45 to 60 seconds. Remove with slotted spoon. Peel off skin. Cut in half from top to bottom. Squeeze gently holding cut side down to remove seeds. Use spoon if necessary. Cut into pieces. Add to onion along with remaining ingredients. Heat. Pour over cauliflower in serving bowl. Serves 6.

CREAM CHEESE CORN

Cream cheese lends its distinctive flavor to this quick dish. White cheese with white corn.

Cream cheese, cut up	4 oz.	125 g
Milk	¼ cup	60 mL
Parsley flakes	½ tsp.	2 mL
Onion powder	¼ tsp.	1 mL
Canned white niblet corn, drained	12 oz.	341 mL

Combine first 4 ingredients in saucepan. Heat until melted. Stir often.

Add corn. Heat through. Serves 4.

Note: Yellow corn may also be used.

SUCCOTASH

Instead of the usual half corn and half lima beans for this dish try this recipe for "Sufferin' Succotash"!

Chopped onion	**½ cup**	**125 mL**
Butter or margarine	**¼ cup**	**50 mL**
All-purpose flour	**2 tbsp.**	**30 mL**
Canned tomatoes	**1 cup**	**225 mL**
Canned corn, drained	**12 oz.**	**341 mL**
Canned lima beans, drained	**14 oz.**	**398 mL**
Granulated sugar	**1 tsp.**	**5 mL**
Salt, good sprinkle		
Pepper, sprinkle		

Sauté onion in butter in saucepan until soft.

Mix in flour. Stir in tomatoes until it boils and thickens.

Add corn, beans, sugar, salt and pepper. Simmer until heated through. If mixture seems to be too thick, stir in a bit of water. Serves 6.

CREOLE STYLE CELERY

Two choices here, with or without thyme. Try both ways. It is like two different vegetables.

Butter or margarine	**¼ cup**	**50 mL**
Chopped onion	**1 cup**	**250 mL**
Canned tomatoes, cut up	**14 oz.**	**398 mL**
Sliced celery	**4 cups**	**900 mL**
Salt	**1 tsp.**	**5 mL**
Granulated sugar	**½ tsp.**	**2 mL**
Thyme (optional)	**¼ tsp.**	**1 mL**

Melt butter in saucepan. Add onion. Sauté slowly until soft taking care not to brown.

Add remaining ingredients. Simmer slowly until celery is tender. Add a bit of water if needed. Serves 4.

CREOLE CHARD: Cut up chard. Use 4 cups (1 L) packed, instead of celery. Works great.

FLORENCE FENNEL

This looks like a short fat stalk of celery. It is cooked much like celery and has a slight licorice flavor.

Florence fennel bulbs	**4**	**4**
Salted water		

Remove stems from top of fennel and cut off bottom. Cut as though you were preparing celery for cooking. Peel outside pieces if needed. Cook in salted water until tender. Drain. Add salt, pepper and butter or margarine. Serves 4 to 6.

Note: To mild out the licorice flavor, serve in Cream Sauce (page 86).

Variation: Sauté fennel in butter or margarine until tender. Sprinkle with salt and pepper.

FIDDLEHEADS

These little ferns are not only delectable but a conversation piece as well. May be served with Hollandaise Sauce, page 84.

Frozen fiddleheads	**10 oz.**	**284 g**
Salted water		
Lemon juice	**1 tsp.**	**5 mL**
Salt, sprinkle		
Pepper, sprinkle		
Butter or margarine, softened	**1 tbsp.**	**15 mL**

Cook fiddleheads in salted water until tender, about 5 to 8 minutes. Drain.

Add remaining ingredients. Toss lightly. Serves 4.

What will it be, a sewing machine or a kiss? One sews seams nice and the other seems so nice.

DILLED PEAS

Serve cold as a salad or hot as a vegetable. Equally good with or without curry powder. Try both to see if you have a preference.

Boiling water		
Frozen peas	**10 oz.**	**284 g**
Sour cream	**¼ cup**	**50 mL**
Chopped green onion	**1 tbsp.**	**15 mL**
Dill weed	**1½ tsp.**	**7 mL**
Salt	**⅛ tsp.**	**0.5 mL**
Curry powder (optional)	**¼ tsp.**	**1 mL**

Pour boiling water over peas to thaw. Drain. If planning to serve hot, cook and drain.

Mix remaining ingredients together. Add peas. Stir. Serves 4 to 6 if served cold and 2 to 3 if served hot.

BEST PARSNIPS

Looks yummy with little pools of butter on top.

Parsnips, peeled and cut	**2 lbs.**	**900 g**
Salted water		
Granulated sugar	**½ tsp.**	**2 mL**
Butter or margarine, softened	**2 tbsp.**	**30 mL**
Salt, sprinkle		
Pepper, sprinkle		

Cook parsnips in salted water and sugar until tender. Drain. Mash well. Spoon into shallow dish. Spread evenly. Make indentations with back of spoon all over the top.

Dab butter in each indentation. Sprinkle with salt and pepper. Serves 6 to 8.

On every Eskimo's Christmas list can be found Christmas seals.

LENTILS

A tasty protein vegetable to serve with a salad or other vegetables.

Butter or margarine	**2 tbsp.**	**30 mL**
Chopped onion	**½ cup**	**125 mL**
Chopped celery	**½ cup**	**125 mL**
Lentils	**1 cup**	**250 mL**
Water	**2 cups**	**500 mL**
Chicken bouillon powder	**2 tsp.**	**10 mL**
Ketchup	**¼ cup**	**60 mL**
Parsley	**1 tsp.**	**5 mL**
Garlic powder	**¼ tsp.**	**1 mL**

Melt butter in saucepan. Add onion and celery. Sauté until soft.

Add remaining ingredients. Bring to a boil. Cook covered until lentils are tender, about 15 minutes. Serves 4.

LEEKS

A delicate onion flavor.

Medium leeks, white part only, cut ½ inch (1.25 mm) thick	**6**	**6**
Salted water		
Butter or margarine, melted	**2 tbsp.**	**30 mL**
Salt, sprinkle		
Pepper, sprinkle		

Cook sliced leeks in salted water until tender. Drain well.

Toss with butter, salt and pepper. These may be mashed at this point, or if desired may be stirred into Cream Sauce (page 86). Serves 4.

She wore a heavy sweater to go to the Mexican restaurant. She heard every time you went there you got chili.

CREAMY DILL POTATOES

Dill weed is speckled throughout this tasty dish.

Hot mashed potato (cook about 2 lbs., 900 g)	**4 cups**	**1 L**
Cream cheese, softened	**4 oz.**	**125 g**
Sour cream	**¼ cup**	**50 mL**
Butter or margarine, softened	**1½ tbsp.**	**25 mL**
Onion powder	**½ tsp.**	**2 mL**
Dill weed	**½ tsp.**	**2 mL**
Salt	**¼ tsp.**	**1 mL**

As soon as potatoes are mashed, add remaining ingredients. Mash together. Put into a 1½ quart (1.5 L) casserole. Keep warm in oven until ready to serve. Makes 5 to 6 servings.

PEAS AND CAULIFLOWER

A simple colorful combination. Added lemon juice gives a wee bit of a nip.

Medium head of cauliflower, broken up	**1**	**1**
Salted water		
Frozen peas	**10 oz.**	**284 g**
Salted water		
Butter or margarine	**½ cup**	**125 mL**
Lemon juice	**2 tbsp.**	**30 mL**

Cook cauliflower in salted water until just tender. Drain.

Cook peas in salted water. Drain. Put cauliflower and peas into serving bowl.

Melt butter and lemon juice. Pour over vegetables, or if you would rather, pour over vegetables combined in saucepan. Toss and serve. Serves 8.

We have kittens to give away. They will do light mousework.

MINTED PEAS

Refreshing. Perfect served with lamb.

Frozen peas	**10 oz.**	**284 g**
Salted water		
Finely chopped fresh mint	**1 tbsp.**	**15 mL**
Granulated sugar	**½ tsp.**	**2 mL**
Butter or margarine, softened	**1 tbsp.**	**15 mL**

Put peas into salted water. Enclose mint in tea strainer or use a cloth bag. Add sugar. Cover and bring to a boil. Boil until tender, about 3 to 4 minutes. Remove mint. Drain.

Add butter. Toss. Serves 4.

Note: To replace fresh mint, use ¼ tsp. (1 mL) dried. More may be used if desired.

PEAS AND LETTUCE

A wonderful combination. The lettuce has just enough crunch. Excellent.

Butter or margarine	**3 tbsp.**	**50 mL**
Chopped onion	**2 tbsp.**	**30 mL**
Frozen peas	**10 oz.**	**284 mL**
Shredded head lettuce, packed	**4 cups**	**900 mL**
Parsley flakes	**½ tsp.**	**2 mL**
Granulated sugar	**½ tsp.**	**2 mL**
Salt	**½ tsp.**	**2 mL**
Water	**½ cup**	**125 mL**

Melt butter in medium size saucepan. Add onion. Sauté until clear and soft.

Add remaining ingredients. Cover. Bring to a boil. Cook about 3 to 4 minutes. Stir once or twice. Drain. Serves 6.

Pictured on page 35.

TOMATO ZUCCHINI DISH

Tomatoes and green onions add color and flavor interest to this zucchini.

Butter or margarine	**¼ cup**	**50 mL**
Chopped green onion	**½ cup**	**125 mL**
Small zucchini, unpeeled, sliced	**3**	**3**
Firm ripe tomatoes, sliced	**2**	**2**
Grated Parmesan cheese	**2 tbsp.**	**30 mL**
Salt	**¼ tsp.**	**1 mL**
Pepper	**⅛ tsp.**	**0.5 mL**
Grated Parmesan cheese	**3 tbsp.**	**50 mL**

Melt butter in frying pan. Add onion and zucchini. Sauté for about 5 minutes.

Add tomato, first amount of cheese, salt and pepper. Taste for salt and pepper adding more if needed. Turn into serving bowl.

Sprinkle with remaining cheese. Serves 4.

Note: To prepare ahead, put into 1 quart (1 L) casserole. Bake uncovered in 350°F (180°C) oven for about 25 minutes until heated through.

MASHED POTATOES PARMESAN

Mayonnaise along with Parmesan cheese adds to the flavor of these.

Hot mashed potato (cook about 2 lbs., 900 g)	**4½ cups**	**1 L**
Finely minced onion	**¼ cup**	**50 mL**
Mayonnaise	**¾ cup**	**175 mL**
Grated Parmesan cheese	**¾ cup**	**175 mL**

As soon as potatoes are mashed, add remaining ingredients. Mash together. Check for salt and pepper adding a few sprinkles if needed. Mayonnaise may be heated before adding so it won't cool potato. Serves 6.

COCONUT RICE CURRY

Good and quite different with the addition of peanuts and browned coconut. Curry is mild.

Long grain rice	**2 cups**	**500 mL**
Chopped onion	**¼ cup**	**60 mL**
Water	**4 cups**	**1 L**
Salt	**1 tsp.**	**5 mL**
Butter or margarine	**2 tbsp.**	**30 mL**
Unsweetened coconut	**¾ cup**	**175 mL**
Salted peanuts, chopped	**½ cup**	**125 mL**
Curry powder	**1 tsp.**	**5 mL**

Combine rice, onion, water and salt in saucepan. Cook covered until tender, about 15 minutes. Water should be absorbed.

Melt butter in frying pan. Add coconut. Sauté until light brown.

Add peanuts and curry powder to coconut. Stir. To serve, mix everything together. An alternate method of serving is to mix half the coconut mixture with rice and sprinkle second half coconut mixture over top. Serves 8.

1. Meatless Chop Suey page 120
2. Fried Rice page 76
3. Pickled Peppers page 104

HODGE PODGE

From the Maritimes and a garden filled with fresh vegetables. This is a fresh vegetable recipe. Amounts may vary according to vegetable preference and to seasoning preference. Great for a barbecue with all in one pot.

Medium potatoes with skin, quartered	**6**	**6**
Sliced onion (optional)	**1 cup**	**250 mL**
Salted water		
Carrots, cut bite size	**1 cup**	**250 mL**
Green string beans, cut up	**1 cup**	**250 mL**
Yellow wax beans, cut up	**1 cup**	**250 mL**
Peas	**1 cup**	**250 mL**
Butter or margarine, softened	**2 - 4 tbsp.**	**30 - 50 mL**
Cream	**¼ cup**	**50 mL**
Salt, sprinkle		
Pepper, sprinkle		

Cook potatoes and onion in salted water until half cooked, about 10 minutes.

Add remaining vegetables. Cook until tender. Drain.

Add butter, cream, salt and pepper. Toss to mix. Serves 6.

SPANISH RICE

Be sure to try this, especially if you have never tried tomatoes with rice.

Long grain rice	**1 cup**	**250 mL**
Condensed onion soup	**10 oz.**	**284 mL**
Sliced mushrooms, drained (optional)	**10 oz.**	**284 mL**
Water	**1¼ cups**	**300 mL**
Butter or margarine	**¼ cup**	**60 mL**
Canned tomatoes, cut up	**1 cup**	**250 mL**

Combine first 5 ingredients in saucepan. Simmer covered until rice is cooked, about 25 minutes.

Add tomatoes. Heat through. Serves 4.

MASHED TURNIP

Just plain and plain good.

Yellow turnip, peeled and cut up	**2¼ lbs.**	**1 kg**
Water	**2 cups**	**500 mL**
Salt	**½ tsp.**	**2 mL**
Granulated sugar	**½ tsp.**	**2 mL**
Pepper	**⅛ tsp.**	**0.5 mL**
Butter or margarine, softened	**2 tbsp.**	**30 mL**
Potato flakes (optional)		

Put turnip, water, salt and sugar into saucepan. Cover and cook until tender, about 35 minutes. Drain.

Add pepper and butter. Mash well. If turnip is watery add potato flakes as needed and mash again. If it isn't watery but too strong in flavor, prepare potato flakes and add the mashed potato to the turnip as needed. Mash well. Check seasoning. Serves 8.

CURRIED TURNIP: Add a bit of curry and mash. Taste and add more if desired. Add slowly. Tasty.

RICE PILAF

Beef consommé rather than chicken gives this its robust flavor.

Long grain rice	**1½ cups**	**350 mL**
Chopped onion	**1 cup**	**250 mL**
Butter or margarine	**¼ cup**	**50 mL**
Condensed beef consommé	**2 × 10 oz.**	**2 × 284 mL**
Salt	**½ tsp.**	**2 mL**
Pepper	**⅛ tsp.**	**0.5 mL**
Saffron	**⅛ tsp.**	**0.5 mL**
Raisins	**⅓ cup**	**75 mL**
Water	**½ cup**	**125 mL**

Sauté rice and onion in butter until browned.

In saucepan combine remaining ingredients. Add rice mixture. Cover. Cook until tender about 20 to 25 minutes. Serves 6.

Note: Saffron may be omitted and ¼ tsp. (1 mL) turmeric added. It won't have quite the same flavor but saves buying the most expensive spice on the market. Raisins may be omitted if desired.

SQUASH AND TOMATOES

Use crookneck or any yellow squash to make this different presentation.

Sliced onion	**1 cup**	**250 mL**
Butter or margarine	**2 tbsp.**	**30 mL**
Yellow squash, peeled and cut bite size	**2 lbs.**	**900 g**
Canned tomatoes	**19 oz.**	**342 mL**
Granulated sugar	**1 tsp.**	**5 mL**
Salt	**¾ tsp.**	**4 mL**
Pepper	**⅛ tsp.**	**0.5 mL**
Basil	**½ tsp.**	**2 mL**
Paprika	**½ tsp.**	**2 mL**
Grated cheese, Cheddar or Parmesan (optional)		

Sauté onion in butter in large saucepan.

Add next 7 ingredients. Simmer covered until tender, about 15 minutes. Turn into serving bowl.

Sprinkle with cheese if desired. Serves 8.

CUSHAW-CROOKNECK: Peel, halve, seed and cut into bite size pieces. Boil in salted water until tender. Drain. Toss with a sprinkle of salt and pepper and a dab of butter or margarine. Brown sugar can be added for a sweet coating.

CHEEZY RICE

A different rice dish obtained simply by adding cheese.

Long grain rice	**1 cup**	**250 mL**
Water	**2 cups**	**500 mL**
Salt	**½ tsp.**	**3 mL**
Grated Cheddar cheese (or Swiss cheese)	**1 cup**	**250 mL**

Cook rice in water and salt until tender, about 15 minutes. Water should be absorbed.

Stir in cheese. Serves 4 or 5.

POTATOES EXTRAORDINAIRE

Make this a day ahead or simply mash and put in the oven to hold about an hour ahead. That way, you are free for other last minute details. Reprinted from Company's Coming Holiday Entertaining. Freezes.

Potatoes, peeled	**5 lbs.**	**2.27 kg**
Salted water		
Cream cheese, softened	**8 oz.**	**250 g**
Sour cream	**1 cup**	**250 mL**
Butter or margarine, softened	**¼ cup**	**50 mL**
Onion salt	**1 tbsp.**	**15 mL**
Salt	**1 tsp.**	**5 mL**
Pepper	**¼ tsp.**	**1 mL**
Butter for garnish		
Paprika for garnish		

Cook potatoes in salted water until tender. Drain. Mash.

Add cream cheese in pieces. Add next 5 ingredients. Beat until smooth and fluffy. Turn into 3 quart (3.5 L) casserole. Make indentations with back of spoon.

Put a dab of butter in each indentation. Sprinkle with paprika. Cover. Heat in 350°F (180°C) oven until heated through. If putting cold casserole into oven, you will need to stir occasionally to prevent outside crusting. Allow 20 to 30 minutes for warm and at least 1 hour for cold. Serves 12.

QUICKEST TOMATO SCALLOP

The most simple of them all. A hit every time.

Canned stewed tomatoes (containing celery, onion, etc.)	**2 × 14 oz.**	**2 × 398 mL**
Crackers, broken up finely using fingers	**12**	**12**

Empty tomatoes into saucepan. Add crackers. Stir. Heat to boiling. To make thicker, add more crackers. Serves 6 to 8.

STEWED TOMATOES

Whether you have a good crop of tomatoes or just want to jazz up canned ones, this will gratify your taste buds.

Butter or margarine	**¼ cup**	**50 mL**
Finely chopped onion	**½ cup**	**125 mL**
Finely chopped celery	**½ cup**	**125 mL**
Tomatoes, peeled and cut up	**6**	**6**
Granulated sugar	**1 tsp.**	**5 mL**
Salt	**½ tsp.**	**2 mL**
Pepper, light sprinkle		

Melt butter in medium size saucepan. Add onion and celery. Sauté until soft.

To peel tomatoes place into boiling water for 1 minute, 2 at a time. Pierce with fork to remove. Remove peel. Add tomatoes and all remaining ingredients to onion-celery mixture. Simmer until tomato is soft, about 10 to 15 minutes. Check for sugar and salt. Add more if needed. Makes about 2½ cups (675 mL).

Note: Canned tomatoes, 19 oz. (540 mL), may be used in which case they need only be simmered long enough to blend flavors and be heated through.

TURNIP AND CARROT

A good combination, especially if turnip is a bit strong to serve on its own.

Yellow turnip, peeled and cut up	**1 lb.**	**500 g**
Carrots, cut up	**1 lb.**	**500 g**
Salted water		
Butter or margarine, softened	**2 tbsp.**	**30 mL**
Brown sugar	**1 tbsp.**	**15 mL**
Salt	**½ tsp.**	**2 mL**
Pepper	**¼ tsp.**	**1 mL**

Cut turnip into same size pieces as carrot or smaller. Cook both in salted water until tender. Drain.

Mash well. Add butter, sugar, salt and pepper. Mash again or beat. Serves 6 to 8.

SPAGHETTI SQUASH SUPREME

A fun vegetable. It may seem intimidating but its a cinch to prepare. May be prepared ahead and heated when needed.

Spaghetti squash	**3 lbs.**	**1.35 kg**
Broccoli flowerettes	**2 cups**	**500 mL**
Zucchini cubes, unpeeled	**1 cup**	**250 mL**
Salted water		
Sliced carrots	**1 cup**	**250 mL**
Salted water		
Cherry tomatoes, halved	**1 cup**	**250 mL**
Butter or margarine	**2 tbsp.**	**30 mL**
Chopped green onion	**½ cup**	**125 mL**
Salt	**¾ tsp.**	**4 mL**
Pepper	**¼ tsp.**	**1 mL**
Grated Parmesan cheese, good sprinkle		

Pierce skin of squash in 6 or 7 places. Set on oven rack and bake in 350°F (180°C) oven for 1 hour, until shell feels a bit soft. Remove from oven. Cool for 15 minutes. Cut in half lengthwise. Discard seeds. Using a fork, lift spaghetti strands with a scraping motion onto paper towels to drain.

Cook broccoli and zucchini in salted water for 1 minute. Cool under cold running water. Drain.

Cook carrot slices in salted water 5 to 6 minutes. Cool under cold running water. Drain. Add to broccoli and zucchini.

Add cherry tomatoes to vegetables.

Melt butter in frying pan. Add onion, salt and pepper. Sauté until soft. Add squash strands and vegetables. Sauté until heated through.

Add cheese. Toss together. Serves 6.

Note: To boil, cut squash in half lengthwise. Remove seeds. Place cut sides down in large saucepan. Pour 2 inches (5 cm) water in pan. Boil covered for about 20 minutes. Drain. Scrape with fork.

Pictured on page 107.

METRIC CONVERSION

Throughout this book measurements are given in conventional and metric measure. To compensate for differences between the two measurements due to rounding, a full metric measure is not always used.
The cup used is the standard 8 fluid ounce.
Temperature is given in degrees Fahrenheit and Celsius.
Baking pan measurements are in inches and centimetres, as well as quarts and litres.
An exact conversion is given below as well as the working equivalent.

Spoons	**Exact Conversion**	**Standard Metric Measure**
1/4 teaspoon	1.2 millilitres	1 millilitre
1/2 teaspoon	2.4 millilitres	2 millilitres
1 teaspoon	4.7 millilitres	5 millilitres
2 teaspoons	9.4 millilitres	10 millilitres
1 tablespoon	14.2 millilitres	15 millilitres
Cups		
1/4 cup (4 T)	56.8 millilitres	50 millilitres
1/3 cup (5 1/3 T)	75.6 millilitres	75 millilitres
1/2 cup (8 T)	113.7 millilitres	125 millilitres
2/3 cup (10 2/3 T)	151.2 millilitres	150 millilitres
3/4 cup (12 T)	170.5 millilitres	175 millilitres
1 cup (16 T)	227.3 millilitres	250 millilitres
4 1/2 cups	984.8 millilitres	1000 millilitres, 1 litre
Ounces — Weight		
1 oz.	28.3 grams	30 grams
2 oz.	56.7 grams	55 grams
3 oz.	85 grams	85 grams
4 oz.	113.4 grams	125 grams
5 oz.	141.7 grams	140 grams
6 oz.	170.1 grams	170 grams
7 oz.	198.4 grams	200 grams
8 oz.	226.8 grams	250 grams
16 oz.	453.6 grams	500 grams
32 oz.	917.2 grams	1000 grams, 1 kg

Pans, Casseroles

8 × 8-inch, 20 × 20 cm, 2L
9 × 9-inch, 22 × 22 cm, 2.5L
9 × 13-inch, 22 × 33 cm, 4L
10 × 15-inch, 25 × 38 cm, 1.2L
14 × 17-inch, 35 × 43 cm, 1.5L
8 × 2-inch round, 20 × 5 cm, 2L
9 × 2-inch round, 22 × 5 cm, 2.5L
10 × 4 1/2-inch tube, 25 × 11 cm, 5L
8 × 4 × 3-inch loaf, 20 × 10 × 7 cm, 1.5L
9 × 5 × 3-inch loaf, 23 × 12 × 7 cm, 2L

Oven Temperatures

Fahrenheit	**Celsius**	**Fahrenheit**	**Celsius**	**Fahrenheit**	**Celsius**
175°	80°	300°	150°	425°	220°
200°	100°	325°	160°	450°	230°
225°	110°	350°	180°	475°	240°
250°	120°	375°	190°	500°	260°
275°	140°	400°	200°		

INDEX

Taste The Tradition

SAVE $5.00

Mail to:
COMPANY'S COMING PUBLISHING LIMITED
BOX 8037, STATION "F"
EDMONTON, ALBERTA, CANADA T6H 4N9

Special Mail Offer: Order any 2 **Company's Coming Cookbooks** by mail at regular prices and **save $5.00** on every third copy per order. Not valid in combination with any other offer.

Please send the following number of **Company's Coming Cookbooks** to the address on the reverse side of this coupon:

Qty.	Title	Each	Total
	150 DELICIOUS SQUARES	$9.95	
	CASSEROLES	$9.95	
	MUFFINS & MORE	$9.95	
	SALADS	$9.95	
	APPETIZERS	$9.95	
	DESSERTS	$9.95	
	SOUPS & SANDWICHES	$9.95	
	HOLIDAY ENTERTAINING	$9.95	
	COOKIES	$9.95	
	VEGETABLES	$9.95	
	MAIN COURSES (Sept. 1989)	$9.95	
	JEAN PARÉ'S FAVORITES VOLUME ONE 232 pages, hard cover	$17.95	
Total Qty.	Total Cost of Cookbooks		$
	Plus $1.00 postage and handling per copy		$
Less $5.00 for every third copy per order			—$
Plus International Shipping Expenses (add $4.00 if outside Canada and U.S.A.)			$
Total Amount Enclosed			$

Orders Outside Canada — amount enclosed must be paid in U.S. Funds.

Make cheque or money order payable to: "Company's Coming Publishing Limited"

. . . don't forget to take advantage of the **$5.00 saving** – buy 2 copies by mail and **save $5.00** on every third copy per order.

Prices subject to change after December 31, 1992.

Sorry, no C.O.D.'s.

Taste The Tradition

SAVE $5.00

Mail to:
COMPANY'S COMING PUBLISHING LIMITED
BOX 8037, STATION "F"
EDMONTON, ALBERTA, CANADA T6H 4N9

Special Mail Offer: Order any 2 **Company's Coming Cookbooks** by mail at regular prices and **save $5.00** on every third copy per order. Not valid in combination with any other offer.

Please send the following number of **Company's Coming Cookbooks** to the address on the reverse side of this coupon:

Qty.	Title	Each	Total
	150 DELICIOUS SQUARES	$9.95	
	CASSEROLES	$9.95	
	MUFFINS & MORE	$9.95	
	SALADS	$9.95	
	APPETIZERS	$9.95	
	DESSERTS	$9.95	
	SOUPS & SANDWICHES	$9.95	
	HOLIDAY ENTERTAINING	$9.95	
	COOKIES	$9.95	
	VEGETABLES	$9.95	
	MAIN COURSES (Sept. 1989)	$9.95	
	JEAN PARÉ'S FAVORITES VOLUME ONE 232 pages, hard cover	$17.95	
Total Qty.	Total Cost of Cookbooks		$
	Plus $1.00 postage and handling per copy		$
Less $5.00 for every third copy per order			—$
Plus International Shipping Expenses (add $4.00 if outside Canada and U.S.A.)			$
Total Amount Enclosed			$

Orders Outside Canada — amount enclosed must be paid in U.S. Funds.

Make cheque or money order payable to: "Company's Coming Publishing Limited"

. . . don't forget to take advantage of the **$5.00 saving** – buy 2 copies by mail and **save $5.00** on every third copy per order.

Prices subject to change after December 31, 1992.

Sorry, no C.O.D.'s.

GIVE  TO A FRIEND!

Please send Company's Coming Cookbooks listed on the reverse side of this coupon to:

NAME ____

STREET ____

CITY ____

PROVINCE/STATE ______________ POSTAL CODE/ZIP ______________

GIFT GIVING — WE MAKE IT EASY!

We will send Company's Coming cookbooks directly to the recipients of your choice — the perfect gift for birthdays, showers, Mother's Day, Father's Day, graduation or any occasion!

Please specify the number of copies of each title on the reverse side of this coupon and provide us with the name and address for each gift order. Enclose a personal note or card and we will include it with your order . . .

. . . and don't forget to take advantage of the **$5.00 saving** — buy 2 copies of **Company's Coming Cookbooks** by mail and **save $5.00** on every third copy per order.

Company's Coming — We Make It Easy — You Make it Delicious!

GIVE Company's Coming TO A FRIEND!

Please send Company's Coming Cookbooks listed on the reverse side of this coupon to:

NAME ____

STREET ____

CITY ____

PROVINCE/STATE ______________ POSTAL CODE/ZIP ______________

GIFT GIVING — WE MAKE IT EASY!

We will send Company's Coming cookbooks directly to the recipients of your choice — the perfect gift for birthdays, showers, Mother's Day, Father's Day, graduation or any occasion!

Please specify the number of copies of each title on the reverse side of this coupon and provide us with the name and address for each gift order. Enclose a personal note or card and we will include it with your order . . .

. . . and don't forget to take advantage of the **$5.00 saving** — buy 2 copies of **Company's Coming Cookbooks** by mail and **save $5.00** on every third copy per order.

Company's Coming — We Make It Easy — You Make it Delicious!

Taste The Tradition

SAVE $5.00

Mail to:
COMPANY'S COMING PUBLISHING LIMITED
BOX 8037, STATION "F"
EDMONTON, ALBERTA, CANADA T6H 4N9

Special Mail Offer: Order any 2 **Company's Coming Cookbooks** by mail at regular prices and **save $5.00** on every third copy per order. Not valid in combination with any other offer.

Please send the following number of **Company's Coming Cookbooks** to the address on the reverse side of this coupon:

Qty.	Title	Each	Total
	150 DELICIOUS SQUARES	$9.95	
	CASSEROLES	$9.95	
	MUFFINS & MORE	$9.95	
	SALADS	$9.95	
	APPETIZERS	$9.95	
	DESSERTS	$9.95	
	SOUPS & SANDWICHES	$9.95	
	HOLIDAY ENTERTAINING	$9.95	
	COOKIES	$9.95	
	VEGETABLES	$9.95	
	MAIN COURSES (Sept. 1989)	$9.95	
	JEAN PARÉ'S FAVORITES VOLUME ONE 232 pages, hard cover	$17.95	
Total Qty.	Total Cost of Cookbooks		$
	Plus $1.00 postage and handling per copy		$
Less $5.00 for every third copy per order			—$
Plus International Shipping Expenses (add $4.00 if outside Canada and U.S.A.)			$
Total Amount Enclosed			$

Orders Outside Canada — amount enclosed must be paid in U.S. Funds.

Make cheque or money order payable to: "Company's Coming Publishing Limited"

. . . don't forget to take advantage of the **$5.00 saving** – buy 2 copies by mail and **save $5.00** on every third copy per order.

Prices subject to change after December 31, 1992.

Sorry, no C.O.D.'s.

Taste The Tradition

SAVE $5.00

Mail to:
COMPANY'S COMING PUBLISHING LIMITED
BOX 8037, STATION "F"
EDMONTON, ALBERTA, CANADA T6H 4N9

Special Mail Offer: Order any 2 **Company's Coming Cookbooks** by mail at regular prices and **save $5.00** on every third copy per order. Not valid in combination with any other offer.

Please send the following number of **Company's Coming Cookbooks** to the address on the reverse side of this coupon:

Qty.	Title	Each	Total
	150 DELICIOUS SQUARES	$9.95	
	CASSEROLES	$9.95	
	MUFFINS & MORE	$9.95	
	SALADS	$9.95	
	APPETIZERS	$9.95	
	DESSERTS	$9.95	
	SOUPS & SANDWICHES	$9.95	
	HOLIDAY ENTERTAINING	$9.95	
	COOKIES	$9.95	
	VEGETABLES	$9.95	
	MAIN COURSES (Sept. 1989)	$9.95	
	JEAN PARÉ'S FAVORITES VOLUME ONE 232 pages, hard cover	$17.95	
Total Qty.	Total Cost of Cookbooks		$
	Plus $1.00 postage and handling per copy		$
Less $5.00 for every third copy per order			—$
Plus International Shipping Expenses (add $4.00 if outside Canada and U.S.A.)			$
Total Amount Enclosed			$

Orders Outside Canada — amount enclosed must be paid in U.S. Funds.

Make cheque or money order payable to: "Company's Coming Publishing Limited"

. . . don't forget to take advantage of the **$5.00 saving** – buy 2 copies by mail and **save $5.00** on every third copy per order.

Prices subject to change after December 31, 1992.

Sorry, no C.O.D.'s.

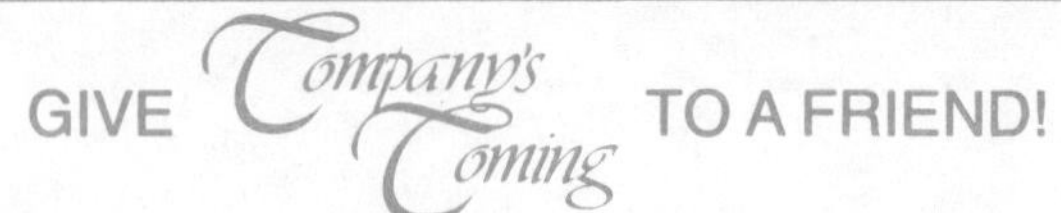

GIVE Company's Coming TO A FRIEND!

Please send Company's Coming Cookbooks listed on the reverse side of this coupon to:

NAME ____

STREET ____

CITY ____

PROVINCE/STATE ______________ POSTAL CODE/ZIP ______________

GIFT GIVING — WE MAKE IT EASY!

We will send Company's Coming cookbooks directly to the recipients of your choice — the perfect gift for birthdays, showers, Mother's Day, Father's Day, graduation or any occasion!

Please specify the number of copies of each title on the reverse side of this coupon and provide us with the name and address for each gift order. Enclose a personal note or card and we will include it with your order . . .

. . . and don't forget to take advantage of the **$5.00 saving** — buy 2 copies of **Company's Coming Cookbooks** by mail and **save $5.00** on every third copy per order.

Company's Coming — We Make It Easy — You Make it Delicious!

GIVE Company's Coming TO A FRIEND!

Please send Company's Coming Cookbooks listed on the reverse side of this coupon to:

NAME ____

STREET ____

CITY ____

PROVINCE/STATE ______________ POSTAL CODE/ZIP ______________

GIFT GIVING — WE MAKE IT EASY!

We will send Company's Coming cookbooks directly to the recipients of your choice — the perfect gift for birthdays, showers, Mother's Day, Father's Day, graduation or any occasion!

Please specify the number of copies of each title on the reverse side of this coupon and provide us with the name and address for each gift order. Enclose a personal note or card and we will include it with your order . . .

. . . and don't forget to take advantage of the **$5.00 saving** — buy 2 copies of **Company's Coming Cookbooks** by mail and **save $5.00** on every third copy per order.

Company's Coming — We Make It Easy — You Make it Delicious!